Beating The Odds

Beating The Odds

❖

82 Years At The Kentucky Derby

John S Sutton Jr and
Amber D Sims

Library of Congress Control Number:		2021919124
ISBN:	Hardcover	978-1-5434-9864-6
	Softcover	978-1-5434-9862-2
	eBook	978-1-5434-9863-9

Print information available on the last page.

Rev. date:03/07/2022

To order additional copies of this book, contact:
Xlibris
844-714-8691
www.Xlibris.com
Orders@Xlibris.com
832567

CONTENTS

DEDICATION

I would like to dedicate this book to my father, the late John S. Sutton Sr., who instilled into me my passion for thoroughbred race horses. Also his father, my grandfather, who handled horses as a blacksmith circa the turn of the twentieth century.

Without their knowledge that somehow rubbed off on the writer, I would have known very little, if any, about the Kentucky Derby and the mannerisms of these magnificent animals.

I thank them both dearly for bringing me along for the <u>ride</u> of a lifetime.

PREFACE

This is a story about a man who has survived various situations—good, bad, and unique. It is about the family that brought about the circumstances that allowed him to be able to attend one of the most iconic sporting events in the world—the Kentucky Derby in Louisville, Kentucky, held now every year since 1875. He has attended the Kentucky Derby for eighty-two consecutive years and counting starting in 1940.

The condition for this race is for three-year-old colts, geldings, and fillies that were nominated and qualified. The qualifications have changed over the years, but was meant only for the top-notch horses (generic) in the USA and later globally.

He is the only person on the planet to have achieved this record. Not only the number of years, but continuously, and also to be present in the paddock to view every horse that has run in that race for eighty-two years.

This came about when he attended the Kentucky Derby with his father when he was eight years old. His father was a thoroughbred racehorse aficionado who studied the lineage, breeding, and genetics of thoroughbred racehorses most of his life. His father—my grandfather—was a blacksmith who owned a horse and carriage shop in Loretta and Elizabethtown, Kentucky. This was the beginning and primary incentive for my interest and knowledge of horses.

At the turn of the twentieth century, most people traveled by horse/horse and buggy, and the maintenance of this means of transportation was essential to civilization all over the world. To my grandfather (Francis Eugene Sutton), this was a means of supporting a family with nine children. This in itself is not significant except this is where the interest in horses was spawned. He shoed rogue draft horses weighing up to 1,800 pounds. His methods were sometimes harsh when the situation demanded, but he had a way of calming these rogues that was second to none. My father spoke of helping his father by holding the horses noses in a twist in order to keep them from tearing up the shop and injuring anyone around. That's where the "Don't get your nose in a twist" originated. He spoke of times when he viewed his father standing in the doorway with sweat pouring down his body and trembling from the exhausting effort of shoeing these powerful animals.

His outlet, as with others of that era, was whiskey, whiskey, and whiskey, especially in that area of Kentucky, was primarily made up of distilleries and Catholics with monasteries and nunneries spread throughout the region when they settled after the Revolutionary and Civil Wars.

As a child, I learned the disposition of horses and their cause for various behaviors from his father. Certain traits carry over to those of the same species. He developed a so-called sixth sense as to their well-being. John Sr. was also valedictorian of his class in high school due to his educated mother (Susan E. Donahue), who tutored him at an early age, being he was the first child. He was chosen by Sister Josephine to represent his county to take a job at the L&N Railroad in Louisville at the age of seventeen in 1919—a worthy prize in those days. To make a long story short, he married my mother (Ruth E. Roby), and I was the second child of three.

My father developed an avid interest in genetics due to his intellect and predisposition in analyzing behavior of both horses and humans. His desire to be an MD was shattered due to the lack of funds and connections, which was mandatory in those days (1920s). This frustration stayed with him along with the hum-drum accounting work he did at the L&N Railroad.

CHAPTER 1

In order to combat these tribulations, my father resorted to increase his consumption of alcoholic beverages, which was a way of life for his ancestors and siblings (not all). Other factors such as an abundance of testosterone (inherited) and his Catholic background forbid divorce and the use of contraceptives, and my mother's reluctance to have more children all contributed to the weekend abuse of alcohol and resentful belligerence. This is only my opinion, but I believe this fight against the male natural desire to breed as nature has dictated is a big factor on self-abuse (or non-self). This incentive drive, coupled with society's demands has been a huge factor in many difficulties associated with society then and now, especially Catholics of the pre-1940s, who followed their faith and teachings and were torn between teaching and inherent instincts. Who wins the battle of the ages, the big head or the little head?

The above observations and facts (family) are necessary here to lay down the basis for the remainder of this book, which gives the reader an insight to some of the unique occurrences and experiences of the author. This endeavor is primarily an attempt to leave a legacy for those who follow. Since I am the last of our clan to know the history associated with this unusual tribe who defied logic because of their self-confidence, which directly led to a bulletproof mentality that resulted in abusive self-behavior. Included in this treatise are legacy verses depicting the <u>favorable</u> analysis of the major players written over a period of fifty years. Some of the <u>shortcomings</u> of human behavior are revealed in the pages that follow.

I suppressed my considerable ego and competitiveness the rest of my life until now at age ninety. I'm joining the me-me world (generation) of the internet such as Facebook, Instagram, Twitter, YouTube, etc., of which I don't participate, in order to satisfy my desire to tell it like it was, then and now. I apologize in advance for tooting my own horn in many occurrences. The reader will notice throughout that I am either <u>bragging</u> or <u>complaining</u>, but I have determined that this reality is essential if the truth be told. What will be, will be.

Francis Eugene Sutton - Age 50 - Grandfather

In order to acquaint the reader(s) with the circumstances, we will start with my earliest memories of my personal life. We—my older sister, younger brother, parents, and me—were renting a house in Louisville, Kentucky, in 1937. As you may well know, the great flood occurred in January/February of that year. We fled our house when the water lapped at our door, as did others. We five and other relatives moved out to the suburbs for shelter at my aunt's house. They could not accommodate all of us, so we moved to Elizabethtown, Kentucky, some fifty miles away to reside temporarily with my grandfather (Gene) and his family. My father commuted back and forth by train for his job at the L&N RR.

By this time, my grandparents' source of money had all but disappeared. Times were hard as the nationwide depression was in full swing, and they were hard-pressed to survive. When the flood waters receded in about a month, I went with my father to see where we had lived and to survey the damage. The waterline ring was six inches from the ceiling and, we lost everything including their Model A in the garage. We rented a house together with my uncle and aunt and stayed there until we could find other residences. Eventually, we ended up near St Joseph's Hospital, in Louisville.

The belligerence began when my father drank heavily on the weekends due to many adverse factors between my mother and father. A vicious cycle had begun between them unbeknownst to us at the time. It was years before I figured out the cause of this trouble. Thus, began the mental abuse directed at my mother by making the children suffer to retaliate against her. Both devout Catholics and forbidden to divorce or use contraceptives or commit adultery, I think, was the primary factor in this unstable situation. I will stop here to partially explain some of the reasons that led to my unique childhood.

Many men dealt with instinctive primal desire to propagate by turning to alcohol binging. My father, John Sr., was graced with robust health with heavy doses of testosterone. This is a perfect recipe for disappointment and subsequent abuse of self and others. Those of lesser health could not indulge in this type of alcohol abuse and quick recovery, which, as I see it, is a blessing in disguise. Of course, this was especially true during the first fifty years of the twentieth century for those who followed their Catholic teachings. Before that, most marriages resulted in ten to twenty children or as many as a woman could have. Homosexuals were almost never heard of but, of course, existed under cover and was rejected by society. Why do the Muslim (Islam) religion allow four wives or whatever? In my opinion, that is why that religion (belief) is and was so popular. Remember the Crusades of the twelfth century as beliefs clashed and war ensued? How did the Roman army become so powerful? Is it partially because their soldiers were driven by their primal desires to enjoy the "spoils of war"? All through history, this was the primary factor in wars. This, of course, is not the only factor, but it plays a large part in the treatise I'm endeavoring to point out.

Since religion in its strictest sense has become less demanding, alcohol now shares this dilemma with *drugs*. I hear many solutions for bad behavior; but the psychiatrists, psychologist, counselors, etc. never talk about this dilemma of all animals, as perhaps they don't really know, but I think I know! Such things fester into resentment and then even mayhem, abuse, or murder. I won't go any further here and let the reader reach their own conclusion, but I will address this human behavior problem later.

My earliest remembrance occurred when I was about six or seven years old, about two years after my brother was born in 1936. On Friday after work and on the weekends my father would stop on at all the taverns in the neighborhood and would not come home until the wee hours of the morning. My father was a typical example of Dr. Jekyll and Mr. Hyde, always snappily dressed with shirt, tie, and hat that were expensive tailored, while we lived very frugally. Fair? Forget it. We moved several times at the insistence of my mother to better herself and the family. The resentment grew deeper as he became more ensconced in debt to pay off, mortgages, etc. His all-night sessions with alcohol finally evolved into an every-weekend nightmare. All, I think, to punish my mother for lack of attention, etc. Of course, his conduct caused my mother to withdraw even further. It was a matter of wills and superseded everything else. He would come in when the taverns closed at 1:00 or 2:00 a.m. on Saturday morning and wake up the whole house and bring us all downstairs to listen to him rant and roar about whatever was on his mind. All directed toward her as she endured his wrath. My older sister and I were made to stay up until the sun came up the next morning. He then continued on up until the taverns opened up and went to visit his relatives. His religion did not allow him to chase women or commit adultery. It was all aimed at resentment and frustration with his "way of life." He could stay awake for three days to apparently prove his point. We all suffered from lack of sleep, etc., especially my sister and me. Later my sister developed an outstanding personality that made her very popular. She tried to stay away on the weekends with her school friends that all wanted to befriend her. She eventually became a social giant that everyone wanted to be with, but I, as the oldest boy, was made to get up whenever he came home and listen to his stories of his youth, work, drudgery, etc. He hated his job because it was so mundane and beneath his expectations and intellect. These nightly (weekend mostly) were exhausting for us children and my mother.

Father - John S Sutton Sr - 17 years old 1920

Soon I adapted to my situation and listened to his musings. That is how I became, following him, the family historian, so to speak. His knowledge of family history was astounding as was his knowledge of current events and thoroughbred races horses. I was exhausted but somehow all this knowledge about life and insights to other peoples' pretentions of being "holier than though" sank in and the intuition that I developed beyond my years.

As the years went by, I stayed up with him to divert his attention away from my mother. As long as he was talking, he would not harass her physically. She endured this abuse because of her upbringing to keep her family together, and divorce was out of the question. To me she was a living saint, and I helped her as much as I could to restrain his attacks over a ten-year period. He recognized my manhood eventually because of my superior strength and fearless attitude. He rested all week after work to get ready for the weekend. This behavior was, by no means, the only situations that occurred. He could stay awake and drink longer than any person I have ever met in my lifetime, and I am not the only person who could tell you that he was a distraction to all his siblings and friends. Why they endured these inconveniences, I'll never know. This, I will attempt to explain in the next chapter.

Before I go on, it is mandatory to know that he worked for forty-seven years at L&N RR in the Auditor of Capital Expenditures office and was very proficient at his job. The Dr. Jekyll side of him was as astounding as was the other side. He also prepared income tax forms for his siblings, cousins, and other kin who were in several businesses. I assisted him to some degree and experienced the frustration that he encountered with preparing these federal/state income taxes for those who were ill prepared and did not furnish the information needed. They thought that he could fix all their shortcomings and that we were mathematical wizards. This, among other misgivings of others, was clearly a contributor to his anxieties and resulted in binges with them after the task was completed. I think we all know that while you are working for whomever (free) and they were sitting at the same kitchen table imbibing, laughing, and talking, it is almost unbearable.

It was not my intention to degrade or upgrade anyone, but state the conditions that led to the unique lifestyle that the author experienced. My mother, who was the principal recipient of this unorthodox abuse, endured by sheer force of her will to withstand this mental torture and whose perseverance and persistence to do the "right thing" won out in the long run. I can still recall her sitting on the sofa with her arms around my brother and me singing, "If I had the *wings* of an angel over these prison walls, I would fly." I would not be alive today if not for her.

I feel as if I inherited my mother's determination and perseverance regardless of the circumstances. I thank her dearly for that. A verse/ poem written about her is contained within this treatise (back pages). She was an RN who received her degree in 1920 with four others. Eventually she went back to nursing at St. Joseph's Hospital as head nurse and took private duty assignments. It was up to me to take care of my brother as far as caretaking, etc. I used to wait for her on the front steps to see her walking (laboriously) up the street with a slight bend because she had bad feet from being on them so much on duty. We would run to meet her, and she would be happy to see us, but not as happy as we were.

CHAPTER 2

Autobiographical Information

"This little life of mine, I'm going to let it shine, let it shine, let It shine." And I hope you don't mind.

Ruth & John Sr. (mom & dad) along with Aunt and Uncle –
Margaret & Jack – Circa 1965 @ Churchill Downs in front of Tote
Board. This is my aunt and uncle that had the farm.

In addition to the circumstances and reasons iterated in the previous chapter, we need to go back to my childhood that occurred other than what has been told. In those days, 1930s to 1940s, etc. our home situated in Louisville was always open (door never locked) due to the fact that my father's siblings, cousins, godchildren, and kin would use our house as a central headquarters, so to speak. We were the only house that had a telephone, and all were welcome to visit during their forays to Louisville. Mostly these stops began on a Friday or holiday, and with them, they brought along their favorite beverage (100 proof whiskey—bottled in bond).

When I came home every day with the groceries, I would see the vehicles parked in front of our house, and I knew what was about to occur. They arrived sometimes at noon-ish to sit at the table and imbibe until my mother and father arrived at 5:00 p.m. Then, sometimes other siblings would arrive and the serious drinking started. This was their entertainment choice rather than movies, etc. (before TV). We never had a car or TV until about 1950. In the meantime, I worked at the corner drugstore as a clerk/delivery boy, which really was a relief until I got off at 9:00 p.m. Then I went home to the rowdy party-goers. My uncle and aunt lived on a farm and always came in on the weekends to John's place, and their son, who was three years older than I, would go to the movies or clubs while they vented their trials and tribulations. Usually around eight or nine o'clock, my uncle Jack would go to the White Castle and Preston and Eastern Parkway and buy enough sliders that they liked; however, my father never ate, usually all weekend. He used calories that were derived from alcohol to sustain him, I guess? After they all left to go home usually about 1:00 a.m., that is when my father would start his verbal abuse and made us all stay up most of them night with his frustrations taken out on my mother. He usually woke up all the neighbors too, but he didn't care. The police were called many times, as were my mother's kin, to stop his ravings. He always convinced the police that he was only exercising his rights and had this polite way (Jekyll) of convincing them that the neighbors were the perpetrators, and they always left us later to his musings. He would lay outside on the hill in the snow rather than come into the house at times. This, all while expensively dressed and always with a Stetson hat. When I come home in the morning, about 6:00 a.m., from my paper route, I would roust him up and we'd go inside. Some of the neighbors also tried to help him in. Why? I do now believe that he tested people to see their real self and ferret out good or bad intentions. Beyond belief maybe, but he sure knew people. In the meantime, all of us were attending school, elementary and or high school. There was no such thing as studying or doing homework at home, and we suffered scholastically for that. In the meantime, other life-changing events took place, especially in my case.

When these weekly episodes took place, I was always right in the middle of their squabbles, fights, arguments, and jokes. Actually, I was called on to perform a few songs that I knew while my uncle danced (two-step soft shoe). He said he learned from Fred Astaire, a noted dancer (movie star). Also an Irish jig of sorts when I sang "Dear Ole Donegal" with all the Irish names that I had memorized. Also they wanted me to recite the "Dark Town Poker Club," which I knew from memory. We only had about six to eight jelly glasses to drink from. Why! Who knows? During these episodes, the men always went to the tavern to purchase and drink more beer, which was at least a respite for the women. Sometimes I went along, but I was reluctant to go and listen to the idiotic palaver. Little known to me at the time, I was subconsciously absorbing human behavior that gave me an insight beyond my years. In the meantime, my sister and brother tried to disappear with the help of my mother. During this era, children were seen but not heard, and hardly anyone noticed what we were doing.

Meanwhile back at the ranch, I was absorbing my father's knowledge of thoroughbred race horses and was learning how to read the daily racing form, since our place was the betting outlet for the group. My interest grew stronger as I listened to the Kentucky Derby race called by Clem McCarthy (noted broadcaster) on the radio. I remember distinctly his passionate commentary about the

1939 Kentucky Derby race, which was won by Johnstown, which my father picked to win. I begged and harassed him to take me to the derby on May 4, 1940. He finally agreed to take me, and we went to the paddock where they saddled the horses, and he pointed out to me some telltale signs that indicated the horse's condition and aggressiveness. I absorbed this quickly, especially since the horse we bet on won and beat the odds-on favorite (Bimelech). After this, I was addicted and acquired as much knowledge that I could from him and DRF. This was the first of eighty-two years of attending the Kentucky Derby, a record as of this writing.

The following year, 1941, we went to the derby, and Whirlaway won and we bet on him. Mr. Long Tail won easily by eight lengths, and he was a beautiful sight to see with his long tail flowing behind him. He was an easy pick, and many people bet him. He later won the Triple Crown. Over his lifetime of racing, he started sixty times (unheard of today) and won thirty-two of them. He was owned by Calumet Farms and trained by Ben Jones. The following year (1942), the derby was won by Shut Out, owned by Greentree Stable. Another easy pick, and we won a little because he was the prohibitive favorite. Interestingly, his dam (mother) was Goose Egg, hence the name. We stayed up all night but still staggered on, and the only thing to look forward to for me was the derby. We moved to a larger house on Keswick Boulevard just a block away.

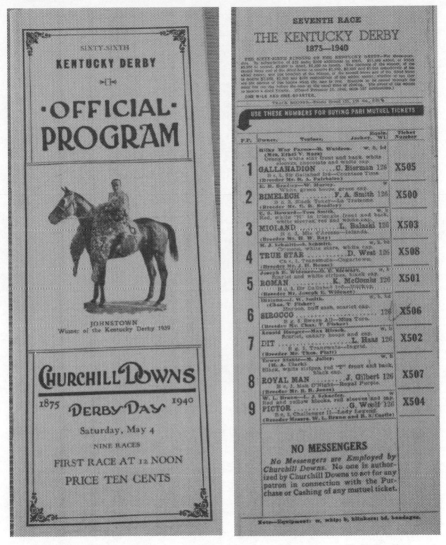

My first ever Ky Derby – 1940 – Program – winner – Gallahadion

In 1943, Count Fleet won the Kentucky Derby on a cold day to no one's surprise. Only nine horses competed against him, and he led all the way around the one and one-fourth mile distance and was the odds-on favorite. No big winnings here. He later sired the 1951 Derby winner Count Turf. WWII was in full swing, and I used to listen to the radio every night with my father for news from the war front from Gabriel Heatter. His opening saying was, "Ah yes, there's good news tonight." The radio and newspapers were the only means of information at the time.

In 1944, Pensive, a Calumet colt, won the derby easily on a cold day and a good track. He was sired by Hyperion, one of my father's favorite sires. He paid $4.60 to show, and we won. Couldn't pass up Calumet Farms/Ben Joes duo. This was when the Kentucky Derby attained prominence as the oldest continually run race in America. Hoop Jr. another Sir Gallahad III offspring, won on a muddy track run on June 9, 1945, delayed from the first Saturday in May because of the war, and he won by six lengths with Eddie Arcaro in the "irons". We lost, but not much, $10 maybe, which was considerable in those days, and I was disappointed. I thought we should win every year. The Belmont Stakes in New York were cancelled because of the threat of war being on the East Coast, where German submarines had loitered off the coast. This was true for a couple of years.

Later that year, when I was fourteen, I had a tragic accident that changed my life forever (discussed later). I had just started high school at St. Xavier three weeks earlier. In 1946, Assault won the derby on a slow track, and we lost and came in fourth or fifth because we bet the Maine Chance Farm entry (two for the price of one). I went to the races on crutches and even played basketball, etc., as it did not occur to me that it was a problem. Oh! The adaptation that youth brings.

In 1947, Jet Pilot won on a slow track (drying out) on a cloudy and chilly day, and we won because we bet Calumet's horse Faultless, and he ran third and paid $4.60 to show—a goodly sum. This was a very difficult race to pick, and we got lucky.

In 1948, one of the greatest horses of all time won the Kentucky Derby on a sloppy track. There was only six horses in the race because of Calumet's two-horse entry who you couldn't bet against. Citation beat his stable mate easily (three to four lengths), and there was no place or show betting. We bet him to win just to say we bet on him (paid $2.80 to win). Citation could run at any distance or any kind of track. He ran forty-five times and won thirty-two of them. He retired to stud in 1949 and did not produce as expected. He returned to racing in 1950 and won five more races and six more in 1951. His sire was Bull Lea out of a Hyperion mare. Outstanding breeding and lineage. Owned by Calumet Farm, trained by Ben Jones, and ridden by Eddie Arcaro. What a combination.

In 1949, Ponder, a son of Pensive (1944 winner), won the Kentucky Derby. We bet him to show ($6.20) because, of course, he was a Calumet colt, and we would have been foolish to bet against Calumet after the success that they had previously. The weather was great, and I celebrated with all.

Middleground won in 1950 and beat some good colts, but we did not bet him anywhere and lost for a change. I was not happy with our research and loss.

In 1951, Count Turf (son of Count Fleet, 1943) won by four lengths and surprised us all. He was a field colt, along with four others, meaning that a bet on the field in those days #12 was a bet on all five. We bet a Calumet colt again but he ran 5th and we lost but still celebrated.

In 1952, Hill Gail, another Bull Lea/Blenheim II, won and led most of the entire one and one-fourth miles. This was an easy pick for us because of the breeding and a Calumet/Ben Jones/Arcaro combo, and paid a surprising $3.20 to show. I was then a junior at University of Louisville and feeling my oats and felt good that I could hardly contain myself, and I therefore set about abusing my body with alcohol and lack of sleep, etc. I was taking premed (three-hours labs) and went every day to school from 8:00 a.m. to 3:00 p.m. and working forty hours per week at Kroger Co. I left class at 2:50 p.m. and punched in at Krogers at 3:00 p.m. (ten minutes later). The first chance I had, I grabbed something to eat—usually a packet of ham and two or three raw eggs and some milk, because I never ate at the university. It's called lack of funds. This was all done on the sly while working. I ate two meals a day for three or four years, morning and afternoon. As a stock clerk, we usually punched out about 11:00 p.m. and went straight over to our watering hole until they closed at 1:00 a.m. I very seldom had time to study, and when I did, it was at school in between classes. I did this for about two years and graduated in June 1953 with a BA in Zoology. It was a fools pace, and I was exhausted and gaunt by that time. More on this later.

Back to the races, Dark Star won the Kentucky Derby in 1953 and beat the great Native Dancer by a head and paid $51.80. We bet Native Dancer to show (entry) and won a small amount ($2.80) but lost on the day. This was the only defeat that Native Dancer suffered out of his twenty-two-race career over a two-year period. He turned out to be a prolific sire, and his progeny was second to none for the next fifteen to twenty years. Native Dancer was roughed up on the first turn and had to check up briefly and was wide down the backstretch. He was closing ground in the end but could not catch the winner.

My second cousin and his buddy who went broke (as usual) on this derby resorted to toe-turning discarded pari-mutuel tickets on their way out, and believe it or not, they found four ten-dollar ($10) place tickets on Dark Star worth $68.00 apiece that had been thrown away, probably by a novice better thinking they were not redeemable because Dark Star had won—unbelievable but true. Pari-mutuel tickets in those days were made of stiff cardboard and could be turned over on the ground by foot/shoe manipulation. This was a rather common practice for losers and apparently paid off to some degree. This was the one and only time that I've seen this kind of luck. They cashed the tickets for $272.00 and proceeded to get even more inebriated, of course, stopping by our house with more whiskey. Just what the doctor ordered—ha ha. So many people who know nothing about racing attend the Kentucky Derby, and that's what makes it so lucrative for professional betters.

Determine won the 1954 Derby with comparative ease, and I arrived in Louisville the night before on April 30 from Fort Sill, Oklahoma, on a three-day pass. My buddy dropped me off in St Louis, Missouri, on his way home to Wisconsin, and I hitchhiked the rest of the way. We bet the Hasty House Farm entry to show, of course, and Hasty Road placed and paid $5.60 to show, so we celebrated again. I left the next day to hitchhike back to St Louis to meet my friend. Again, my father's knowledge of bloodlines proved to be invaluable.

The reader may wonder why we always bet to show heavily and bet a very small amount, $2 or $5, to win or place. One must remember that the Kentucky Derby offered a unique opportunity to win money to a knowledgeable punter and with greater number of horses in the race and 90 percent of the spectators betting on names, numbers, etc. played right into our hands and increased the show payoff to almost double to what was the ordinary payouts. The competition in racing is the other betters, and the house (track) just takes its cut regardless of who wins or loses. In fact, they want the favorites to win because more people win and thus continue to bet the next race, so to speak, which in turn give the house more moola! Competing against others was always my forte and made the juices flow—it's called gambling fever.

In 1955, Swaps won the derby and beat the great colt Nashua. Swaps was only the second horse bred in California to win the Kentucky Derby. You might say this was the beginning of notoriety for California-bred thoroughbred horses. We bet Nashua who appeared to be a slam dunk, so to speak, and he ran second and paid a paltry $2.40 to show, so we just about broke even. Swaps was trained by M. Tenney, an unorthodox trainer who legged his steeds up by running them on the sand beaches in California. Nashua was the son of a prolific sire, Nasrullah, and went on to have a winning career.

Needles won the 1956 Kentucky Derby. He was a come-from-behind type and the public liked this kind of horse because it was so thrilling to watch. The weather was clear and perfect for our entourage, and we enjoyed the day. We bet Fabius (entry), a Calumet colt ridden by Willie Hartack, who went on to win five derbies. Fabius paid $3.60 to show, and we celebrated on into the night again. We just could not bet against Calumet in those days of yesteryear.

I attended the 1956 Derby even though my wife, who was pregnant, had an operation to remove an ovarian cyst and we were staying at her father's house. She was more or less bedridden for the remainder of her pregnancy, and she wanted me to go to the debry, I think, just to get rid of me for a while, ha ha.

CHAPTER 3

By the time I was twelve years old, I could study the racing form before and after the race better than most adults. By the time I entered high school, my family relied on me to read the form and give them my opinion (even my father). My ability to focus intently on that and blot everything else out was a godsend. I did not want to study my schoolwork, and my grades did suffer somewhat. I did all my homework at school while others were doing mundane things. I had absolutely no interest in girls during this phase, and that left me with an open mind to do as I pleased. I was left to my own devices and could come and go at will. I was small for my age ninety-five pounds and five feet two inches at fourteen due to not eating right, even though my mother insisted. I wouldn't stop playing basketball on the side street of our house where we erected a hoop and banking board on a telephone pole. People from the surrounding neighborhood all came out to play because of me having a basketball (leather), which wore out quickly on asphalt. My dear and Louisville prominent Uncle Eddie (Edwin Roby), who was the owner of the Edentide team, a semipro team, played along with the Phillips Oilers, Fort Knox Tankers, etc. That was before the NBA, and they were the top players in the nation. They played their games in Louisville at Columbia Gym on Fourth Street near downtown. I used to sit on the bench with the players and would shoot balls during halftime. Uncle Eddie gave me the old balls that were no longer in use. I dearly loved him for that!

It must be stated here that from a 95-pound weakling with a damaged foot, I transformed myself to a 170-pound physical specimen that few dared to mess with. This was way before the exercise craze later on, and I was the only one that exercised to any degree other than running and playing baseball, football, basketball, etc. I was determined to fulfill my mission of being able to protect myself and others.

I did this by innovating different methods and objects to build muscle, etc. I lifted concrete blocks down in the basement, where I was sent when I misbehaved, and sewer caps (ugh). Soon I was the only one who could lift a sewer cap with one hand above my head. Doesn't sound like much, but it bolstered my physical superiority among those present.

At night, we (three or four) went out hunting how we could mooch free beer. I must tell this following story: Lighthouse Lake was a swimming pool situated on Gardiner Lane on the outskirts of Louisville. At night, all the lifeguards (supposedly muscle men and ladies men) would assemble on the sand where they had barbells for weight lifting to show off to the adoring females who occupied the scene. One would try to outdo the other to gain their ladies' attention. Since I was around six feet and 170 pounds, I appeared to be thin and not strong. We took advantage of this oversight to humiliate the big boys in front of their girlfriends. I would bet a beer for all of us against their top strong guy (they thought). I knew how much weight was on the barbell and knew that I could press that above my head. They thought they were the only ones that could do that. In contests, I waited on the sideline for them to get to their maximum weight— about 180 pounds for so. Then I would step forward and bet that I could lift that weight overhead. Our group (three or four) appeared like scraggly itinerates and that we were below their status. Har har!

I would bet beer for all of us against one for them to see if I could lift as much as them and their sought-after adulation from all around. A perfect setup for me. I reveled in the opportunity to embarrass the so-called bullies/he-men and put them in their rightful place. This is the attitude that I adopted for the <u>rest of my life</u>, and it's what made me a natural-born leader. Everybody wanted to be my buddy! In any event, they (he-men) took me up on my challenge and thought I was easy pickin'. I would stall long enough to fool them into thinking I was just some punk who dreamt a lot. They all had to eat *crow* when I was able to hoist (press) 180 pounds above my head, more than my body weight. Later they barred us from coming into their little private enclave, so we snuck in one night after they went inside to do <u>whatever</u>, and we removed all the weights and barbells, which I think belonged to Lighthouse Lake. I took them home and used them for years and taught my sons how to gain strength, and I still have some of them today. To the victor goes the spoils. I was unconcerned with all my accomplishments (if you want to call it that) and suppressed by evolving ego so that I wouldn't offend others. This is just one of many incidents where I achieved my goal of knocking down the bragging egotist to teach them a lesson; some never forgot. My mother was well pleased because I didn't brag. Now at my age, I have abandoned that philosophy, as you can plainly see. I waited a long time!

It's at this time that I developed a disposition and a demeanor that, when in a competitive situation that required a judgement of others as to ones ability, tended to for them to underestimate me and make rash decisions that, in the end humbled them. I reveled in helping them to arrive at a wrong decision and to re-think their rash judgement and to eat crow, so to speak.

I only practiced this tom-foolery when I was in contact with the egotistical know it all's. This enticement, however, did not always prove to be advantageous, but it was a part of my attitude, good or bad. This in turn, made them reluctant to confront me in the future. Naturally, as all egotist do, they rationalized their mistake and justified their flimsy insight. This peculiar characteristic enabled me to make good lasting friends like Bob, Bill, Jim and Herb who never practiced this undesirable chest thumping trait.

Basketball and horse racing were all I cared about at that time. I was the starting guard for the Bloodhounds team and was a charter member of that city team. We won the city championship when I was thirteen years old, and I was sure bet to star in high school 1945–1949; however, a life-changing event occurred first when I entered St. Xavier High School at fourteen years of age. On September 24,

1945, I was involved in an accident coming home from a paper route that me and a friend had. It was my last day on the job. We both had quit because of school, which involved morning and evening delivery of the newspaper. The *Louisville Times* and *Courier Journal* was a daily paper, and we really didn't make enough money to keep it up. This accident, a streetcar ran over my foot, and I almost lost my foot and/or leg. The recovery from this took about a year. I was hospitalized for two months with a cast up to my hip. This, of course, put me way behind in school because as a freshman in high school, it was the worst time due to the introduction of Latin, algebra, etc. I spent the rest of my school years trying to catch up. I still don't know why they didn't let me skip school that year and start anew next year. My foot became infected after they removed my crushed great toe. Subsequently, to make a long story short, I received the first skin graft (taken from my left thigh) in the city. Sulfa drugs did not contain the infection, and penicillin was just beginning to be used was given to me in large doses (too much). This resulted in a case of large welts (hives) that was worse, as far as suffering was concerned. I came home in December 1945, and I remember by sister crying when she saw me. I weighed ninety pounds and looked like a starving refugee. It took two months of constant Epsom salt bathing by my wonderful mother to keep me from dying. Once the infection broke and the swelling subsided (size of a football), I went back into the hospital that required fifty-five stitches to attach a skin graft to the ball of my foot. My dreams of playing sports came to an abrupt end, and this was when my life changed for the better.

I was left alone because everyone was working, and I had time to think about my future. I, of course, went to the Kentucky Derby that May on crutches. I knew that my life was going down the drain, and I started exercising with anything I could find—mostly concrete blocks that were in the basement. I began eating more so that I could gain some weight. Things looked pretty bleak for about a year. I started to see the results of my makeshift exercising program, unknown to anyone.

My father, in the meantime, continued his drinking and would even bring other drinkers he had met at different taverns to show them my leg/foot. My left leg had atrophied from being in a cast, and I tried to bring it back to life, but it never came back to the size of the other leg. However, my patience and my mother's care encouraged me to carry on as if nothing had happened.

Since I was a quick study in sports, it enabled me to pick up and innovate to help myself. In short, I grew eleven inches in one year with strong arms. My arms were already strong from making fires with twisted newspapers each morning, since my father would let the fires go out overnight. C-O-L-D. To start a coal fire without kindling wood is hard to do, and my forearms became powerful from the force required to twist the paper so it would stay lit log enough to start the coal burning. Sometimes it required two or three attempts with proper drafting, etc. I even had to start our neighbor's fire (two older ladies) and soon quit that because after the first week, they gave me a thin dime (10¢). That was the end of that.

In the meantime, the weekly parties of alcohol venting continued as before with the same routine. Everyone was lamenting their tribulations and resulted in long arguments, fights, and crying jags. I don't know if the reader has ever seen or heard a crying jag, but it is something to behold. They always ended up singing "Sweet Adeline," "When Irish Eyes Are Smiling," and "Let Me Call You Sweetheart" before departing about 2:00 a.m. The night had just begun for us as my father continued on until we were all exhausted. Truth is sometimes stranger than fiction. Everyone suffered as a result of this insane behavior.

In those days, if you were a Catholic, you could go to the parish and take the *pledge* not to drink for a year or whatever. My father did this about two different times as I recall, a slight respite occasionally. Things were said and done during the weekly forays that would take up too much time to read and absorb.

I somehow managed to grow stronger both mentally and physically, but my brother did not, unknown to all of us. There was an old Sycamore tree outside our house and, ever since I was able to reach the lower limb, I never went past it coming or going without doing ten to fifteen pull-ups. This, I think was primarily responsible for the development of my latissimus dorsi muscles in my back and gave me a forty-four-inch chest and a twenty-nine-inch waist later when I was eighteen. Quicker and stronger than anyone around, along with a fearless attitude, was a real asset and served me well all my life. A slender build of 170 pounds.

My mother encouraged me to help others and rebuke bullies, which I did, and she was proud of me. I would do anything she asked, which wasn't much, except to be successful and respect others.

Money, of course, was always a huge factor, and even though we lived in a middle-class neighborhood, all my friends seemed to have enough money to exist on. I sold my father's beer bottles for two cents per bottle to go to the movies on Sunday. Later, I paid the price after he discovered they were gone, but that did not deter me. He refused to pay for my Catholic high school education, and I was called out of class every other week to be ridiculed. He had obtained his great education for free, as he put it, and thought that was the way it ought to be. After being called out of class, I adapted to this ridicule also and really didn't care anymore. My siblings did likewise. I went to work at the corner drug store as a delivery boy and earned $5 weekly, of which most went to tuition. I again adapted and plodded on with my feet hardly hitting the ground. I felt so good I could dismiss almost anything. I just thought that was the way it was; it was very hard to embarrass me. The drug store cowboys who hung around at night would try to harass me but found it not rewarding, for I knew how to reciprocate to older males who attempted intimidation. I simply could not be bullied! This may all sound like I am bragging, but to tell the story, these things are essential for understanding my psyche. My natural leadership characteristics were starting to take hold without me even trying. My daredevil persona was still there, but with a lot more caution. This is not to say that I was wise enough to avoid other potential hazards. At seventeen, everyone wanted to be my friend, and I tried to befriend most. I don't know why this came to pass, but since I treated everyone good, I thought, and took up for those who were left behind, so to speak, as my mother had taught me.

There were some that challenged me, but in a boxing, or wrestling engagement, they were no match, and I always left them off the hook without embarrassing them much. I would fight any injustice that occurred and would always settle for a <u>draw</u>, this way no one got hurt, including myself. This was the era of fighting to settle an argument—hardly anyone had a gun in those days. My, how times have changed.

I graduated high school and had the wanderlust of "go west, young man, go west." My buddy, Cliff C. and I decided we were going to Yellowstone National Park via hitchhiking with duffel bags and a train ticket to St Louis provided by our parents, both RR employees with free tickets. Needless to say, this was a real learning experience about life. When we got back, I went straight to the hospital with pneumonia.

I went to work at Paramount Pickles where my uncle got me a job. I think this was a setup because they wanted to teach me a lesson. They put me on the toughest job in the factory. When I came home on the streetcar each day, I would sit in the back while everyone else moved to the front. The vinegar/pickle juice smell permeated everything. I was so tired when I got home, I took a bath and went straight to bed. My tough guy persona was shattered. Good lesson though.

I had no intention of going to college, but this changed my mind. I went to U of L, took a test, and was accepted. No one knew, but I had to tell my mother, and she was happy. She dug up enough money to pay for my first semester, which was $184. I got a job at Kroger Co. nearby as a stock clerk for the next four years and paid my way through the rest of college. I took premed, simply because my mother was a nurse and had no counseling, orientation, or any advice. I worked from three to eleven most days and twelve hours on Saturday. When you take chemistry, physics, and biology, there are always three-hour labs that were attached. I did not study except when I was at the university waiting for the next class to start. I went through a year of physics and didn't even have a book. My extra money, other than tuition, was spent on beer and such. I would not have existed if it weren't for beer, whiskey, and fortitude. In the meantime, the Korean War had started, and I was deferred until I graduated (BA in biology) because of my premed course. Many of my high school mates were killed in that war.

In the meantime, I was home about five hours out of the day. I started dating a neighborhood girl, and she helped me tremendously to carry on and graduate. I graduated in June and was drafted and inducted into the army in August. I could not bear to lose this wonderful caring girl that I was dating. She was so different than the others, with a hefty IQ and work ethic and an inside and out beauty. Why she liked me, I will never know. Opposites attract, they say, and it was so true. We got married in December after basic training. We had a four-day honeymoon, and I went to Fort Knox for five months. The army had so many inductees at that time it was a real problem to find a place for them. We were assigned to an idle barracks to wait for orders to ship out. There, we policed the area and played games, mostly poker and wrestling on old mattresses laid down in a large room. For some reason, most of the guys migrated to me, and I certainly didn't persuade them. I won almost every poker game, which was great because I was married. These people that played were rash amateurs relying on <u>luck</u>, whereas my experience with educated players was proficient. I wrestled all comers and lifted some weights most of the time. I was determined to make myself stronger for the tasks that lay ahead. One stocky German kid thought he was God's gift to physicality, and we wrestled every day. He couldn't understand why I was so strong because, of course, he thought he was the best. He never gave up trying to beat me, but never did. I always left him off the hook, so to speak, because I didn't want him to be embarrassed. Anyway, it passed the time until I was shipped out to Camp Chaffe, Arkansas, near Fort Smith, Arkansas. There were thousands of guys there awaiting further assignments, and I stayed there about a month.

I forgot to mention that while I was a Fort Knox, I was assigned to <u>Wire</u> school, which consisted of climbing telephones poles, using telephones and switchboards, etc. Why? Ask the army. When I first went in, we took IQ tests, so to speak, and I was signaled out to attend OCS (Officer Candidate School), but I refused because if I had accepted, I would have had to sign up for an additional two years of duty. I hated the army chain of command, and I rebelled at everything they did. I couldn't accept someone less intelligent than I and telling me what to do, and that audacity will always remain within my psyche. However, I was clever enough to keep my mouth shut and just meet the minimum requirements. I wanted out of the army and counted the days since I first was drafted. Many others were court martialed for failing to obey orders and were sent to the stockade.

John Sutton -Wire school - US Army

Meanwhile, the Korean War had ended with a shaky truce, so maximum wartime training was in effect. I eventually was assigned to Fort Sill, Oklahoma, and joined the 216th Field Artillery Battalion, Company B. This battalion was the sole possessor of the 280 mm atomic canon, which could shoot twenty-five miles. I was assigned to a survey team as a computer (manual) due to my mathematical aptitude. It was sure better than being a taper or whatever. It was our job to secure the coordinates for the huge canon emplacement. This was done, in those days, by a triangulation with a theodolite (transit) from geodetic points, etc. In any event, it was an easy task for me, and I made a lot of lifelong friends there. Unfortunately, we were sent on a grand scale maneuver to Fort Bragg, North Carolina, and resided in pup tents for three months with a constant fear of coral snakes, which populated that pine tree area where we pitched tent. Unknown to me the first lieutenant of our survey team kept all my manual calculations and later revealed to me that he only found one incidental mistake among thousands of logarithmic interpretations, and he was amazed by my thoroughness and accuracy. He said he'd never encountered a person like me and later wanted me to go to Germany with the 216th.

I can't finish here until I tell the reader of the two friends that I made, who slept next to me in the next cots. There were characters deluxe. While others on the base went to Lawton, Oklahoma, each payday ($78 per month) and spent all their monies, we instead traveled in my friend's car to Wichita Falls, Texas, just across the Red River Border (fifty miles). The purpose, of course, was to bring a carload of real beer back to the barracks to have each day after work had ended. The temperature there at Fort Sill hovered around 100 degrees every day during the summer, and it was almost impossible to sleep on the second floor barracks without being drenched in sweat. Instead, the three of us motored to the Wichita Wildlife Refuge almost twenty miles out of Fort Sill. We went up the highest mountain (hill) and enjoyed the cool breeze and the real beer. Oklahoma only sold 3.2 beer, which was no use to us. We would come back around 4:00 a.m. to stand call at reveille at 5:00 a.m. Others in our Company B begged us to sell them a cold beer, but we wouldn't part with even one beer. It was all we had to look forward to at the end of each day. All three of us despised the army because we were rebels against authority, and these many beers helped us to overcome our attitude. We could easily dispense a case of beer in one night, but rationed it out to last a whole month.

Sergeant R. was our survey leader and had his own quarters in a little room at the end of the barracks. I noticed he had made some barbells made out of concrete buckets that he would work with after the day's work. I stopped by and talked with him, whom I admired, and watched him bench press lying on his footlocker, and he finally got around to asking me if I wanted to try lifting. I said I'd like to try, and so I did.

It wasn't a whole lot of weight, I'd guess 100 pounds or so, but it was so easy for me I disregarded it, so to speak. When I bench pressed it five or six times, he was shocked, again by my slim appearance. After several sessions, he asked me how many times I thought I could bench press that weight. I nonchalantly said ten or fifteen times, and he didn't believe it. I made sure I bragged on him and his desire to improve himself. A couple of days later, he asked me to try and see what I could do. I knew from past experience not to appear too anxious. In any event, I finally did it and bench pressed that weight fifteen times, and he was amazed. He had other buddies in other companies with the battalion (1,000 men) that exercised, etc., and word got around. Later, he asked me to arm wrestle, and I stalled long enough that he thought he would, at least, overpower me with his two-hundred-pound frame.

He, of course, thought that he would outdo me in this endeavor. This was my specialty, and I had never lost an arm-wrestling contest. I knew better to humiliate him in front of his underlings, so I toyed with him, and it ended in a stale-mate. I knew right away that I could win. Carefully, over several sessions, I couldn't fool him any longer and I won. All this time, my demeanor was one that I had cultivated over the years. I was twenty-two years old, and my mannerisms and real persona was one of an <u>unassuming</u> and an unconcerned person, and I downplayed my abilities with self-deprecating mannerisms, which was actually genuine.

He had told all his cohorts about me, and they wanted to see to believe. His buddy in Company C was the battalion arm-wrestling champ (1,000 men). He was six feet five inches and weighed 230 pounds. They invited me out to a downtown tavern in Lawton for drinks (beer). I didn't have any money, but they didn't care. In a booth opposite each other, we set up our challenge. He was confident he would win. To make a long story short, we battled to a draw using either hand. They bought me all the beer I could drink, and I enjoyed the game. He and I were then proclaimed co-arm wrestling champions of 216th Field Artillery Battalion, and everybody was happy. I would like to say here that I did not advertise this or mention it ever again until now. After this episode and display of strength, everyone respected me even more and made my life a lot easier. At age ninety, I am now changing to fit into the me-me generation, mainly to hand down my legacy to those kin that follow so they may benefit from what their genetic inheritance was or could be and to sow confidence in them, which is so important.

Later, my wife Doris joined me to live off base in Lawton, and she applied for a steno job at Fourth Army Headquarters on base. Starting out as a lower GS Grade, of course, within three weeks they promoted her four grades because of her dictation and steno skills. I heretofore have not mentioned her intellectual ability (above mine), and she, too, was unassuming and considered her skills to be ordinary with a beautiful disposition. She genuinely cared about others and was a joy to be around. I look back now and marvel at how fortunate, or lucky, I was. You must remember here that it was 1954, and recorders and all the tech stuff were not in play at that time. She was one of only a few on that base who could take dictation from several higher-ranking officials in classified meetings simultaneously. This was beyond my comprehension, and they paid her well and promoted her immediately for this special skill set.

The 216th was ordered to go to Germany, and since I had only eight more months to serve my two-year hitch, I was not eligible to go. You had to have nine months or more to go before you could go overseas. This proved to be a dilemma for Company B. They were not only going to lose me but also my wife. They begged both her and me to re-up for three years so I could go with them, because by then, I was a survey team instructor and leader and expert in setting coordinates for the atomic cannon (280 mm). They even threw a party to convince her and me to go with them, but I was having none of that because I wanted to get out of the army in the worst way. My mindset at the time was one-sided, and my stubbornness was unequaled. I tried all my later life to change this Sutton trait but was only partially effective. By the way, this was not my only shortcoming, because I had a penchant to ignore other people and so on and so on. I could not accept being told what to do by someone inferior to my mentality or physicality. This would prove to be detrimental to me over the years to come.

I came home on leave on a three-day pass (hitchhiked) to attend the Kentucky Derby just because that was what I wanted to do. I had no idea at that time that I would end up attending eighty-two derbies.

Back to my wife, Doris, for a moment. She was a studious A student in a Catholic elementary school and continued on in a Catholic high school for girls and achieved the highest general average for four years in high school and then attended a business school and completed their course in half the time it took others. She did that partially because her financial situation was dire, because her father had lost his job because the company closed down. She was college material, but did not have the funds to pursue that end, and the scholarships in those days were few and far between, and also, I think other factors were in play at the time.

Her perfect cursive penmanship (Palmer method) was exactly the way it was meant to be. No flare or special letters, so what does that <u>say</u> about her? She was, like me, severely underestimated early on and proved a lot of people wrong in their rash judgments, which served as incentive for both of us. Again, the last laugh!

My hectic and frantic childhood was in total contrast to her quiet, steady, and organized household; therefore, she had what I was seeking—some peace and stability, and she provided that in spades for me. What a good Catholic beautiful girl saw in me as a wild undisciplined bad boy is beyond me. Anyway, opposites attract, I suppose—thank God! Our time together at Fort Sill was a happy one for me, and she helped me endure the army's punishment for not re-upping. They sent me to the 332nd Corp Battalion, who were going on maneuvers, so during that time I had to leave her alone in Lawton while I went to Fort Hood, Texas. This was my second at playing war games (maneuvers), and I didn't like it at all. In any event, I served my time in less than ideal conditions and was in charge of a Jeep returning from the field. My driver took a right-hand turn on a gravel road, and we (four men) flipped over several times. Thank God the roll bar was up at the time, or we would probably been killed or severely wounded. They blamed the incident on me for letting him speed, etc. They wanted to charge me for the Jeep, $1,200 at the time, so I lied my way out of it, and the other three men backed me up. They knew better but couldn't <u>prove it</u>. Three months later, I was honorably discharged because my time was up. This was the third time I had rolled over in a vehicle, one end over end; once when I was nineteen and survived without a scratch—another reason to write my legacy. It was meant to be that my fate hung in the balance many times, and I was lucky to be alive.

Before I go on, I need to explain here what was responsible for my physicality. Between the ages of ten to fourteen, I was constantly in motion and played every game I could. Small among others, I could compete favorably in any endeavor. I was so busy trying to win every challenge that I never ate properly and that, coupled with all night sessions that my father made us endure, wasn't ideal, but it made me quick and elusive; and few could catch me and mostly competed against older kids. I could do anything well. Ninety-five percent of the time, I was on the winning side because I had a winner's attitude. I was marble champion of the whole area and ended up with about six thousand marbles, which I won from others. My father taught me how to hold a marble and shoot. After one session, I picked up his pointers. I also could juggle, hand stand, walk on my hands, and do other mundane things. The reason for stating this here was because it was instrumental in developing my confidence, and I <u>thought</u> I could do anything (ha).

After my serious accident, as previously stated, I embarked on a mission, and confidence helped me to grow physically; coupled with the strength I had acquired, as mentioned earlier, it made me a winner. Even with a slightly handicapped foot, I didn't give failure a second thought, and a steady perseverance molded my life to excel in whatever I did. With this positive attitude, I was a force to be reckoned with. I went from an undernourished quiet kid to just the opposite. My relatives all thought I wouldn't amount to much, and I was assumed to be the one less likely to succeed. This also spurned me on. I was reticent early on and took a back seat, so to speak. The lesson here is to <u>believe in yourself</u> and don't be deterred by others' opinions and assumptions. Of course, later everybody jumped on the bandwagon. My mother always, and later my father and sister, saw the light.

CHAPTER 4

Unknown to me, my younger brother (five years), while I was in the army, had a <u>severe</u> nervous breakdown while he was a senior in high school. They did not inform me of this until after I came home from service. His survival hung in the balance, and only his inherited characteristics enabled him to survive. It must be said that he was also very good at physical sports and was normal in every way. I didn't realize that my departure would affect him so drastically. This took the wind out of my sail. We always played together, and he was also proficient in most things but never acquired enough confidence. I think my sudden departure affected him, and I neglected to see his situation even though I don't know what I could have done. He depended on me more than I thought, and I never got over this misfortune. To my father's credit, he took him under his wing, and he took him with him on his weekend meanderings, and my brother loved it. They even traveled to New York to see Jack Dempsey at his restaurant, and of course, he was not there (too old), but they drunkenly demanded to see him, and they were kicked out. Just one incident of many more to come. This is another story in and of itself.

After my discharge, we had no idea where we were going to live, do or die. Two days after my discharge, I signed up for a course in organic chemistry at U of L because in order to be eligible for dental school, this was a required course. I finished in about five to six weeks. There was one spot open for dental school, and I took a manual dexterity tests with three other candidates. I was accepted and had to put up $100 to secure my seat in September 1955. I soon realized that this was a pipe dream because we had very little money to pay tuition, etc., and I would not been able to work and attend dental school simultaneously, so I forfeited the $100. I had not thought the whole situation through, obviously.

In the meantime, my father purchased a small tavern in the west end of town and wanted me to run it because he was not yet retired. His dream, I suppose, because he had spent enough time in those establishments.

Meanwhile, we had moved in with my wife's parents and paid $50 per week to them for food and shelter. I was hardly home, just to sleep for about four to five hours. I worked in the stupid pub fourteen hours a day and on holidays, trying to make it work. Even with my work ethic, it wasn't enough. I did this for about a year before I told my father I was done. We couldn't make any money because there was a tavern on every corner that sold cold beer for two for 25¢, a cost loser. My wife also worked for a cheap attorney, and we were hard-pressed to eke out a living. She got pregnant in December 1955, and at five months, she had to have an ovarian cyst the size of a large orange removed. She had to be off her feet for the remainder of the pregnancy. Fortunately, we were living with her parents, and that was a break. A beautiful auburn-haired daughter was born on September 5, 1956, and all was in good health. We moved into a low-income HOA that same month. I also obtained a job at a major company on September 17, 1956, as a materials quality control technician, making $72.50 a week. Probably the lowest-paid job, except the mail boy. I, however, was so thankful for the job that I jumped in with both feet. My boss was impressed with my work and liked me. He once stated that with his brains and my constitution, he could have been president of the USA. He was a chemical engineer with a big ego and reckless demeanor. He was also impressed by my knowledge of thoroughbred racing and the Kentucky Derby. He was from Mississippi, and he had very little exposure to racing. He was also in charge of whiskey filtration and losses and had frequent encounters with government gaugers who supervised whiskey making and made sure the Treasury of the US was getting their $10.50 per proof gallon tax at that time. He was one of the smartest persons I had ever met, but everyone hated him because of his overpowering ego and attitude, but he produced and that kept him in his job.

He recognized my mathematical aptitude, and he and I set out to further our education. He didn't care what others thought and plowed on, and since he was so productive with his ideas, they kept him in that job until he became untenable due to many other factors, etc.

We had two other sons, all in thirty-five months, and this was a nightmare for both of us. After that, I holstered my gun because the doctor told me that another child could be disastrous for my wife.

As usual, my feet just hit the ground on every other step. Driving a fenderless 1950 Canadian Dodge that my best buddy lent to me and driving on banana skins, I had a flat tire every other week. I could change a tire in about five minutes, while others I worked with passed me up on the way to/from work. I forgot to mention that I smoked cigarettes since age fifteen and drank booze at an alarming rate of consumption, but I could recover very fast, and it didn't affect my output, except my wife wasn't happy.

This was where I realized that I was about to follow in my father's footsteps. I could, and did, get by sometimes on one or two hours of sleep and a gin and lemonade on the way to work. My buddy could not believe that I could do this for years. He iterated that he had never seen anyone like me! Good and bad. Always, at every chance going to the race track—Churchill Downs, Miles Park, and Keenland. I was an expert and couldn't resist the thrill of gambling and thoughts of making a few bucks.

With my knowledge of horses and his (my boss's) desire to make more money, we surmised that if we had enough past statistical data, we might come up with a beatable system of wagering. I told him that I saved my money to make what I would call a big bet on derby day to *show*, and since I had been successful at that, our research centered on a <u>show</u> bet theory.

I left work at three thirty and went to the main library on York Street and went back ten years and obtained race results from Churchill Downs using microfiche files of the *Courier Journal* newspaper to calculate facts on favorites to show in allowance races. When we obtained enough samples over a period of time, we analyzed it to see if we could turn a profit by betting the favorite to show in the feature race of the day. This took several months, and it revealed it was more or less a break-even situation. So we each put up $100 to bet to show when the races at Churchill Downs were in town (spring and fall). I would leave work and rush out to Churchill Downs to make the bet. You would walk in free after the seventh race, so it just cost my time and effort, plus gas. After two years, we gave up this idea that it was a moneymaker. However, the research that we did added to my knowledge of how to bet, etc. There are two significant points to winning at the races. #1 is to pick the right horse and #2 how to bet that selection (called Money Management).

Of course, I attended the Kentucky Derby each year and had bet on the 1957 Iron Liege, 1958 Tim Tam, and 1959 Tommy Lee winners to <u>show</u> and was flying high and sort of giddy. I was brought down to reality the next couple years, but still, I retained my enthusiasm and had an extreme amount of focus, built up over the years of studying the racing form, etc. This we primarily did at my parent's house on Saturday when the races weren't in town. In those days, there was a bookie on every corner, and we had access to all of them. It was open-house again on the weekend, and horse betting was at the center of our activities. My father, my mother, friend, cousins, etc., and I bet at almost every track that was running at the time, mostly Arlington, Keenland, Fairgrounds (New Orleans), Florida tracks, and all the New York tracks (three or four). We thoroughly enjoyed this endeavor. We limited out bets to what we could afford, and a celebration was in progress regardless of whether we won or lost. Unfortunately, we drank to excess and carried on into the night. I now had my father, brother, friend, and myself to contend with. This created a hardship on my wife, but it did serve to protect my mother from any verbal abuse. The whole arrangement was a mistake, and it was wrong to participate in this senseless activity. How I managed to survive in that was a minor miracle.

My service in the company as a Materials Quality Control

manager included the presence of a son or daughter during the summer of one of the executives or friends. They justified summer work for their offspring to learn about different incremental parts of the company to have them earn money to acquaint them with what life was all about. A worthy cause indeed, unless you had to train them and they were not an asset. Most of them were willing to work, but, of course, someone had to show them what and how to do the work. Guess who coddled these young people from 1960 on through the thirty years of my tenure? I didn't think anything of it at the time. Not one of their parents or them ever thanked me even though it was considered part of my job, which no one told me about. Their help was insignificant, and I had to tutor them, so to speak. If they came to work later for the company then their three-month stint counted as one full year of longevity, which was an added benefit for them. In the mid-60s, one young man was assigned to me, a son of a well-to-do family of the scientific school at the University of Louisville. They all liked me because I treated them as individuals and not special. He admired my know-how and physical prowess since he was taking huge doses of testosterone pills. He asked me if I wanted one marble-sized pill (horse pill), and I said I did not and in no way needed to boost my libido. I think he learned more from me in three months than ever before. He invited me to meet his parents and to lunch, and I politely refused because I wasn't looking for any connections, etc. Maybe I was wrong, but my mindset (heritage) was to not <u>want</u> or <u>need</u> any help. I was young, virile, and independent to a fault—so be it. The only person I accepted any degree of help from was my first boss, whom I talked about earlier.

One incident that I'll never forget, among <u>many,</u> was across the street from the Bottling House. There was a hardware store with living quarters upstairs. My lab was on the fifth floor with a view of most of the neighborhood (not the best), and during the hot summer, the occupants had to have the windows open or die of heat stroke (no AC). To make a long story short, a man and woman lived in this upstairs apartment, and he would come home from work about 3:30 p.m., and she was waiting for him stark naked, all three hundred pounds of her, and they would have sex right there and then. Everyone watched from our site across the street, and it was a sight to be behold. He weighed maybe 125 pounds, and he could barely hang on to perform his manly duty, ha. It was like riding a bucking horse, and to this day, I can still see it in my mind clearly. It was so hot even with a fan blowing on them that it was a slippery performance, and he was overjoyed to see that show—well, we all were. I've got to give these performances five atta-boys for action above and beyond the call of duty. I have many more tales that are hard to believe that I will try to describe later.

In the meantime, I was taking math classes at the University of Louisville at night with my boss. He and I both knew we weren't going anywhere without an advanced degree, so I actually had to fulfill my undergraduate math requirement to be eligible for acceptance to graduate school. I did this off and on for about six years—no easy feat with a forty-plus-hour work week and three children in diapers at the start. A pipe dream turned into a godsend as to my promotability down the road. I eventually received my master's degree in mathematical statistics from U of L. All my family were surprised when I told them I was going to receive a degree because I never even told them I was pursuing such an endeavor. They were completely unaware I was attending these difficult classes at night. In order for the university to teach such a curriculum, at the time, you had to have at least ten people to sign up for the #600s classes, and this was a problem because mostly my boss had to solicit people to attend in order to make the number required to teach a class in graduate math. That was no easy task. At least two of the people dropped out after two weeks, but our teacher, Dr. R. I. Fields, continued on. He was a math professor at the Speed Scientific School at U of L, and he was brilliant. He kept six games of chess going all the time with some of his colleagues.

How I managed to keep all these balls in the air was hard to believe. I couldn't have done it if not for my past life, that built confidence that I could do anything. Also my wife somehow was able to endure all the escapades and was devoted to taking care of the

children. On weekends, I would workout with my sons and attend
every Little League ball game of both, attend my daughter's dance
recital and took my sons to guitar lessons. It was a rat race deluxe,
but somehow we pulled it off. All this time, I was consuming alcohol
at an alarming rate, coupled with smoking. I fully expected to be
dead before age forty. I had access to all the booze I wanted and
spent very little money on booze and nothing on myself because I
didn't care about spending money. I was extremely frugal because I
learned at an early age to be able to do without. Most of the time, you
have to learn to do without before you can do _with_. My friend Bob, at
the time, was even more frugal than I because his family had to do
without in order to survive. In the meantime, I was working hard at
my job. The harder I worked, the better I felt. I worked hard, drank
hard, and played hard with seemingly very little consequence.

John and Tom Sutton - John 32 years old - Tom 4 years old

1962 Easter Pic of John, Doris, Debbie, Gene & Tom

CHAPTER 5

My boss took a job at Pratt and Whitney in Florida, and I was promoted to materials quality control manager in 1964. I continued to attend the races at Keenland and Churchill Downs in the spring and fall and had a goodly sum bet on Northern Dancer to show in the 1964 Kentucky Derby. In those days, and before you could take in with you at the Kentucky Derby, almost anything you wanted—such a booze, chairs, chaise lounges, coolers, umbrellas, food, etc.—our group took all our supplies with us and arrived early at 9:00 a.m. to obtain an advantageous spot in the clubhouse near the paddock so we could view the horses being saddled, etc. We usually had passes to obtain entry, but it wouldn't cost much to enter anyway, <$5. My father, mother, Bob (my friend), cousins, and myself made up this group. One of the few enjoyments was on Derby Day once a year.

We still lived in a community project with all utilities paid, and now I had enough money to live on, barely. To back track a little, after my return from the army, in addition to my other activities, I helped many people with their problems. Somehow, everyone looked to me to help solve their problems. As if we didn't have any! I didn't refuse anyone because it was my MO to do to so. Money, psychological, or whatever, I tried to help and did. We were living day to day and trying to save money to purchase a house, but this never came to pass until 1981. I refused to pay the high interest rates banks wanted to pay off a mortgage. I watched my father and his siblings and others struggle with paying off thirty-year debts and knew the dire straits this put them in, and I was beyond stubborn on this subject. It was hard enough to just have the secondhand transportation that we needed to and from our constant transportation needs. My friend Bob was a jack of many trades, and he took his time to help me with any repair that was needed, whether it was cars, washing machines, or whatever; and after each repair or fix, we celebrated by drinking what I furnished, and we had some good times together. I don't know what I would have done if not for Bob. We could have a good time on fifty cents or sometimes nothing ($0). He knew all the tricks to save money, and I learned a lot from him. At times I regret the hardships that I caused to my family, especially my wife, who stood beside me through everything as she had always done after I first dated her. She believed in me and my strength of mind and body. Not many, or none that I knew of, would have endured these sacrifices she had to make to carry on. The best decision I ever made was marrying her that fateful day of December 12, 1953, after basic training. We had to get a special dispensation from the bishop in order to get married during Advent (Catholic holy days) and were together for four days on our honeymoon to Gatlinburg, Tennessee. We borrowed her father's 1948 Ford auto to make the trip. We weren't together for four months after that until I met her in St. Louis, Missouri, on a three-day leave. Time together was sparse until she came to Fort Sill to be with me almost a year later. These were the happiest days of my life.

I now had money to obtain what a family needed, and things were much better even though I continued my frugal ways. At work, I ate in the cafeteria every day while others went elsewhere to eat, which cost at least double. One person that worked under me in the lab went out to eat quite frequently, and I guess his mother was subsidizing him. Back tracking for a moment, when I first started working as MQC technician in 1956, I ate lunch for 10¢. There was a small grocery store on the next block (in a poor neighborhood) that would sell you a thick slice of bologna with two pieces of white bread and a thin slice of cheese and put mustard on it for a dime. I ate there twice a week and drank whiskey and water to wash it down. Even my boss sometimes ate with me. I couldn't understand how these other people could waste their money on more expensive food for the same amount of nourishment. Eventually, they all went bye-bye to other places, I guess.

Also, during this time in the late '50s, I had become an ace troubleshooter for the production line whenever it broke down, and I was in charge of whiskey losses, which, if not kept in check, was a big loss to the company. At the time, the federal tax on 1 proof gallon of 100 proof whiskey was $10.50 per gallon, and excess losses really added up. Under my supervision, the losses were cut in half. I feel as if I was <u>undercompensated</u> for this achievement, which lasted almost twenty years. When production took it, the losses immediately tripled; I wonder why? I, in fact, was a one-man show, with one helper. The harder I worked, the better I felt, and hangovers only lasted about an hour, and I never had a headache or any other ill effects from drinking the night before and sometimes with three or four hours of sleep. My constitution, as my first boss and Bob indicated, was superb, and I knew it. The reasons for this, in my opinion was (1) genetics, (2) confidence, and (3) early childhood (fifteen years old and younger) self-taught physical and mental concentration and determination eventuated by the unfortunate tragic accident I stated previously.

CHAPTER 6

I bet on Iron Liege to show in the Kentucky Derby in 1957 to take on Gallant Man, the favorite. This was the famous derby where Willie Shoemaker mistook the 1/16 pole for the finish line and stood up momentarily and came in second. The reason I bet Iron Liege was that he was owned by Calumet Farms and trained by Ben Jones, who were dominant at that time, and was sired by the great Bull-Lea and Sir Gallahad III bloodlines, thrice removed or three generations back on the distaff side—my father's favorite bloodlines. I think Gallant Man was the better horse, but I was betting to show, of course. He paid $6.20 to show, and I was ecstatic. This was followed up by Tim Tam in 1958 (Calumet Farm) on a muddy track. This was the derby that Silky Sullivan was in and who had captured the hearts of racing fans all over the country for his come-from-behind victories in some prep races, but I knew that he wasn't the class of horse to beat the others, especially on a muddy track. He always started way behind and had to make up too much ground against better horses. He finished way back and was never a factor. So ended the saga of Silky. Again, my father's knowledge of lineage and bloodlines proved to be the deciding factor in our winning. We again bet First Landing to show in 1959, which he did, and paid $4. Tommy Lee was the winner, and we broke about even.

In 1960, Venetian Way won the Kentucky Derby on a cloudy day and on a good track and was ridden by Willie Hartack and paid $14.60 to win. He fooled a lot of experts, including us, and we bet Tompion to show, but he ran fourth. We lost but drowned our sorrows in our favorite booze.

Carry Back won the 1961 Kentucky Derby with Johnny Sellers in the irons on a track listed as good and paid $7 to win. There were fifteen colts in the race, and Carry Back came out of the fourteenth post position. He literally came from last to first, and it was a thrilling race to watch. He was owned by a colorful owner/trainer, J. A. Price, and was bred in Florida. He was not of royal breeding, and we bet Crozier to show and he ran second and paid $4.20 to show, and we were back on the winning track again and celebrated as usual.

On May 5, 1962, Decidely won the Kentucky Derby on a fast track and on a pleasant day. He was ridden by W. Hartack and paid $19.40 to win. He was the son of Determine, the 1954 Kentucky Derby winner, and had good breeding credentials. We bet Ridan, the hot favorite, and he paid $3 to show; and we broke about even and went about our customary celebratory ritual.

Chateaugay won the 1963 Kentucky Derby for Darby Dan Farm on a fast track and a pleasant cloudy day. He was ridden by B. Baeza and paid $20.80 to win. We bet Never Bend, and he paid $3.40 to show. He was owned by W. Galbreath and trained by J. P. Conway. There were only nine horses in the race, and the winner came out of the first post position. We won a small amount and did our thing!

Also, in the mid-60s, a tragedy took place in the production building that shocked everyone. A label supplier was a frequent visitor in order to address problems we had with labeling, and he had been given freedom to come and go as he pleased. A female employee was working in a small cubicle on the third floor keeping track of special numbering of our brand labels, and she has been there for some time even prior to my arrival. They apparently were having an affair for some time. She was a single attractive, likeable woman, and he was a middle-aged and married man. She apparently wanted to back out of the relationship, but he became angry over the situation. In any event, he walked in one day after lunch and shot her as she sat at her desk. He then shot himself in the head. I was in the vicinity and heard the shot but had no idea what it was with all the other noise that was always present on the production lines. The police/ambulance pulled up to the front door, and they were carrying her out on a stretcher, and she yelling, "Help me! Help me!" She died on the way to the hospital. I was standing by the front door and next to the shooter, who had a handkerchief blotting the blood from his temple. He later also died. What a catastrophe! After that, a guard was posted at the front door, and no one entered unless they were approved and signed in.

I would like to iterate here that I mostly was focusing on the racing form while others were having fun and socializing. Concentration at the racetrack has always been my forte, and it's the only time I completely forgot life's tribulations, and it was fun for me. This intense focusing at the track allowed others to socialize and then turned to me when it was time to bet. It seemed like the more I drank, the more I concentrated. The motivation here, of course, was that I didn't want to lose *money*.

It must be mentioned the many variables that are associated with trying to pick a winner and a novice will not succeed if they do not know the conditions of the race always stated in the program or racing form. This, in itself, is mystifying for an off and on punter. Most people do not want to exercise their brains to deal with the many variables to consider and deploy other means of determining their betting selection. There are many so-called experts that offer their advice in the program (track handicapper), racing form (several and consensus of all of them). There is no shortage of advice when it comes to your selection. For instance, my mother, whose specialty was the Daily Double, had her own methods and left the nitty gritty up to Dad and me. She subscribed to what used to be called the Blue Book, which reported in "horses to watch" at many tracks, and she religiously followed that advice and was able to come up with some long shots occasionally. I think the reason she liked to play the Daily Double was because of a more lucrative payoff, and she hit them quite often and became known as the Queen of the Double. In those days, there was no such things as exotic betting, i.e., exactas, trifectas, pick 3s, etc.; and the Daily Double only consisted of the first two races of the day. Her picks were always considered by me. As your probably know, there is nothing more thrilling than to be standing in the smiling line at the cashier window.

To those unfamiliar with the history of racing, they had different windows for betting and cashing. There were betting windows for $2, $5, $10, $50, and $100 for win, place, and show at some tracks, plus across the board windows for that particular bet of first, second, and third combination. The same was true for cashing, and you always had to stand in line to bet or cash. This required many tellers to man these windows, and they were situated all over the clubhouse and grandstand. The great expanse of the largest racetrack (Churchill Downs) required a large workforce and on Oaks and Derby Day and the Infield, where all the partying went on—and I do mean excessive drinking, dancing, and playing. Racing was secondary to the inhabitants of the Infield, but accounted for a larger attendance. In fact, it was in some ways said to make the Kentucky Derby so popular for the younger crowd. I could go on and on about what happened there, but there is not enough time to describe the debauchery that occurred. Good for the soul, I suppose. I only went to the Infield one time in my eighty-two years, mainly because you could not concentrate at all, and losing money was almost a sure thing. And we were too serious to partake of these shenanigans. Our after-track partying was more fun for us, and we, Bob and I, celebrated whether we won or lost. These years of the '40s, '50s, '60s, and '70s were the heyday of racing in America.

Like I stated previously, there was a bookie on every corner or block. It was supposedly against the law, but that was almost laughable, for the law enforcement was practically nil since payoffs were a way of life at the time. It was a great time to be alive, and the excitement it ignited was addictive. I would not trade those days for anything even though living was hard for most of the dwellers. It was the *buzz* times.

Incidentally, we went to Keenland outside of Lexington during their short meets at every opportunity. Since the Keenland meet was just prior to CD meet, it was advantageous to us because most of these horses that ran at Keenland came to CD to run. Keenland was in the heart of thoroughbred race country and was built to accommodate the horses owned by the large horse farms populating the area. It is still one of the most picturesque tracks in the country, and if you haven't been there, it has got to be on your bucket list. In those days, they did not even have a track announcer, and no race was called to post or announced. It started out as a track for the big horse farms owners to train and race their pricey horses.

In 1963, Chateaugay won the Kentucky Derby for Darby Dan Farm, owned by J. W. Galbreath, former ambassador to Great Britain. There were only nine horses in the race, and we bet No Robbery, who ran fifth after being in contention, but faded in the stretch. We lost but celebrated anyway.

The torrid pace that I had set for myself during my college years continued, but not with the same stress factors. I had completed my graduate degree in mathematics courses and set about trying to write my thesis—a big undertaking for me at the time. Choosing a subject that has not been taken by others was not easy for me. Dr. R. I. Fields, my counselor and teacher throughout the last four years, was very helpful, and I thank him for that guidance.

He had a very difficult later life because his wife has several maladies, and he had to take care of her almost constantly. I would go over to his house nearby for consultation and advice, and I could hear his wife moaning and calling for him while I was there. I saw dishes piled up in the sink, and the place was a mess. I didn't know how he carried on, and he was an inspiration to me. That's when I knew how lucky I was. He had managed to survive regardless of his situation. The next time I came over, I brought him a quart of whiskey, not even knowing that he drank it, but I figured it may help him endure his crosses that he bore without complaining. He was a brilliant man that was saddled by unfortunate circumstances and passed away years ago.

When I took my oral exam, it was a trying experience. Those present to grill me was Dr. Spragens, head of the mathematics department, a biology professor (my minor), Dr. Fields, and *me*. While I was explaining parts of my thesis, I noticed that the biology professor was doodling on his notepad and had drawn a sword with blood dripping from it. Reassuring to say the least. In any event, I passed and received an A on my thesis. Thank the good Lord that ordeal was over and I could try to lead a normal life.

I set up an exercise program for my sons, Eugene and Thomas— eight and nine, respectively. We used to do the daily dozen out in the yard, and they seemed to like it. I was trying to prepare them for the obstacles that lay ahead. They were involved with a Little League baseball program, and we practiced pitching and fielding quite often. They also had access to a basketball court and were good players. Gene played for Holy Family basketball team and was their star player in the seventh and eighth grades. Thomas was also a good player but lacked the knowledge of the game. I worked with Tom on his pitching, and he became the only pitcher who could pitch strikes in the eight- to nine-year-old league. He later pitched and batted for his thirteen-year-old team. He had become a very strong kid because we lifted weights and started at an early age. Gene was naturally big and strong and considered our exercise program a waste of time and effort.

Meanwhile, our oldest child, Deborah, was a delightful little girl; however, when she was a baby, she cried a lot, and we and the doctors could not figure out what was wrong. She outgrew this to become one of the cutest, sweetest, mannerly little girls; and everybody loved her just as they do today. People used to comment what a well-mannered little girl she was. Thank God she had her mothers' disposition. More about this later.

In 1964 Northern Dancer won the Kentucky Derby for Windfields Farm and was bred by E.P. Taylor (a Canadian). There were 12 colts in the race including Hill Rise, the favorite with Willie Shoemaker up, and he as trained by H.A. Luro. The track was rated fast on a pleasant day. He was sired by Nearctic out of a Native Dancer mare. He had number 7 post position and was away alertly and near the middle of the pack through the 1st six furlongs while under restraint and moved up quickly at the mile pole to take the lead and prevailed by a neck over Hill Rise. He was ridden by W. Hartack and went on to win the Preakness and ran third in the Belmont Stakes. He set a new track record of 2:00 flat for the Derby. He retired after that and became one of the most prolific sires of champions of all time. We split our bet between him and Hill Rise and collected on both tickets, but did not win much due to low show payoffs, $3.00 and $2.60. This was a great race to see due to the duel down the stretch. Make mine a d-double.

Lucky Debonair won the Kentucky Derby in 1965 by a neck over Dapper Dan, a thirty-to-one shot, and from that moment on, I always tried to bet a $2 to win on a long shot with our big bet to show. The weather was perfect, and we had a grand time picnicking on the grounds in front of the paddock tote board. We lost, but not much.

In 1966, Kauai King, a son of Native Dancer, won the Kentucky Derby and led all the way of the one-and-one-fourth-mile distance. He was ridden by Dan Brumfield, a local jockey, and was the favorite. My father picked a rather long shot and bet him to win and place. He was seventeen to one and got up for second and payed $13 to place. Again, his bloodline knowledge was evident. We all won, and the weather was great, and we had a good time.

In those years, my mother, Ruth, went with us and kept us in line. Also, my brother Richard, who had that severe emotional or nervous breakdown, as it was called in those days, accompanied us; and he was still hard to deal with, but my father catered to him and looked after him. We all tried to help, but he was the principal caregiver. He and Richard would ride around all night, keeping all his kinfolk hoping he wouldn't knock on their doors at 3:00 a.m. on a Sunday morning. This continued for many years, and Bob and I were with them most of the time. Why? I am unable to explain that behavior. Even Sigmund Freud could not psychoanalyze the reason for this type of behavior. Drinks, talk, and drive was a big waste of time, but that was the modus operandi at the time. Another unique debilitating pastime that no one else attempted that I know of.

In 1967, Proud Clarion won the Kentucky Derby and was our crowning moment of all the derbies. We were at Keenland when Proud Clarion ran second in the Bluegrass Stakes, then ten days before the derby, we noticed that he was not extended and would probably be fresh for the derby. I studied the racing form all night and decided he could be bet. Before that, I had told all my coworkers he was going to win. This was a bold statement, but everyone voiced their choice. The problem, of course, was the great horse Damascus was the heavy favorite, and I was not taken seriously even though they knew that I knew quite a bit about horses. Betting against Damascus was a difficult decision, but Proud Clarion was sired by great distance runners Hail to Reason and he, in turn, was sired by Turn-To. By this time, we were not on a shoestring, and we could bet a little more than usual. We scraped $20 together and bet Proud Clarion to <u>Win</u> and Damascus to Show $100. We figured this was a chance to win big. We felt sure that Damascus would at least show, and we would get our money back if Proud Clarion lost. A strategy we often employed. Proud Clarion was trained by Lloyd Gentry, who was sometimes thought of as an eccentric. It had rained on Oaks Day, and with a slight drizzle on Derby Day, Gentry made a statement that Proud Clarion did not particularly like an off track, and I think that's why he went off at 30–1. The track was listed as *fast*, but it was only *good* at best. Barb's Delight was on the lead for 1 3/16 miles, and Damascus was well positioned with Proud Clarion back in the pocket early on. Proud Clarion caught Barb's Delight at the 1/16th pole and won by a length; and Damascus closed, as expected, to take third. We were ecstatic and couldn't really believe what had just happened. Celebration deluxe did ensue. Finally, our knowledge paid off big time for us. I had bragging rights at work, but downplayed the recognition, which made it even more substantial; and from that day forward, I was always asked who was going to win the Kentucky Derby. My buddy Bob bought a riding lawn mower and painted Proud Clarion on it. This also inspired my father to write a small book about how to bet thoroughbred racehorses. More on that later.

CHAPTER 7

By this time (1964–1968), I was reporting to a new boss, the main laboratory manager. He was frustrated also because they had promoted a doctor of chemistry over him, and he (the doctor) did nothing but set foot in the lab and read MAD comic books. He liked me and left me alone to do my job, and I was happy with that situation. He would come over to our Materials Lab every day about 3:30 p.m. and sit in my chair behind the desk, and I would listen to his philosophies. I think he just wanted to get away from the establishment's eyes and ears. He was a Republican precinct captain and espoused hard right ideas and policies. I disagreed with almost everything he said, but I remained silent because he was a decent and well-meaning person. He was biased beyond belief and considered Adolf Hitler to be his hero. Figure that one out if you can! It shows that you can be an educated, well-liked person and still hold deep-rooted prejudices.

Going back to when I was hired in 1956, our sales came mostly from one brand. I survived a 10 percent cut in personnel in 1957. I thought I was a goner and had my hat hanging by the door. In 1958, the company was fortunate enough to purchase an iconic brand for just a few million dollars, and that was the single most important acquisition the company ever made. Even today, it is a global leader in sales and profit for the company. The Personnel Department became the Human Resources (HR) around the mid-60s and meddled in everybody's job description, pay evaluations, and conduct. They grew more influential over the years and patted you on the head while kicking your ass out if they determined you are not of their liking. This was the start of the politically correct era. Psychology and philosophy, Jesus!

In 1967, they hired Bill, a Purdue graduate to assist the packaging manager, who was an engineer. It wasn't long before the packaging manager left because of various misdeeds, and Bill took over that job and was very prolific and turned out twice as much work and accuracy as his predecessor. He was well-liked and interacted with me as MQC manager out of necessity. We soon became friends and enjoyed each other's company, and it wasn't long before he also could see that some of our leaders were lacking.

During these years, the chairman and CEO became ill and were decent men. Imbibing at the time had been and was part of the corporate culture, and I think that contributed to their eventual demise. They were the grandsons of the founders of the company and stayed that way for about forty more years and is still controlled by them. The Production Department was handled by a stern tactician engineer that led by fear and intimidation, and it worked. He hardly spoke, but could look a hole through you, and you wondered whether you had egg on your tie or whatever. Of course, everyone was trying to get promoted as human nature dictates, but if you weren't an engineer, your chances were slim and none. He was a fan and owner of a few thoroughbred race horses, and when he found out through the grape vine that I picked Proud Clarion, he at least would talk to me but hardly anyone else. I think he could see in my eyes that I could not be intimidated or bluffed and had no fear in him or anyone else, which I carried over from my younger days. I was not interested in any promotion on top of that. I was happy where I was and what I was doing. Even at corporate Christmas parties and other gatherings, he would stand alone, and everyone was skeptical to converse with him. Any way he did talk to me about horses, and others couldn't believe that I was one of the few underlings that he would talk to. His horse won the Junior Derby at Miles Park, a leaky roof track (minor) that ran at the old fairgrounds property. He then purchased a highly bred animal named Ruffinal, sired by Ribot. He was aware that I knew my horses, and I managed to have a decent relationship with him. In any event, he was highly excited about his new colt and had high aspirations for him and was in training as a two-year-old and put him in some impressive workouts, one of which was spectacular, that caught the eyes of the experts, so to speak. He went 3/8th of a mile in thirty-three seconds and change, where thirty-six seconds for that distance was considered good. He was elated, and that's the first time I saw a light in his snake eyes. Later, Ruffinal pulled up lame before he began racing, and his dreams were shattered. Into each life, some rain must fall. Later, he became president after the second family owner member passed away, which I previously mentioned. At the time, he was telling me about his colt's misfortune. I could see his eyes glisten with a slight tear. It was then that I knew that behind that hard-faced portrayal of himself to others, he really did have some feelings, and the fear factor was all an act and he was vulnerable underneath the veneer he presented.

In 1968, Forward Pass was declared the winner of the Kentucky Derby even though Dancer's Image actually won the race, but was later disqualified because of finding a prohibited medication, except for pari-mutuel payoffs. Bob and I were standing near the entrance to the paddock from the track (tunnel), as usual, as the horses were brought over from the backside (barns). When they came into the tunnel, we saw two attendants take the wet wraps off Dancer's front legs and splash them with a bucket of water. We knew that he had sore legs and had been standing in ice and was enough to bet against him, even though he was a great horse; so we bet our old Calumet standby, Forward Pass, to win. Ironically, they paid the people that had Dancer's Image, and we lost our money because the Dancer wasn't disqualified until the next couple of days. I thought I had seen it all, but that took the cake! A little disappointed, but not enough to keep us from celebrating anyways. The weather was pleasant, and the track was *fast*. The beat went on at home and at work, and we maintained our good-time ways in spite of very little disposable monies. We could have a good time on very little money spent— maybe $1 apiece on a fish sandwich we bought across the street from the track at Veterans of Foreign War Legion Post. That was our usual sustenance on any day at the track.

My job had actually turned into a troubleshooter on the production line and subsequent written reports to the satisfaction of all. In the meantime, the Christmas parties became rowdier and fun for the employees. In 1968, I went with another glass supplier rep to Marion, Indiana, to inspect a new bottle production. Al was a tall, dark, and handsome guy who had survived many harrowing experiences, and he was a pleasure to be with. In those day, the supplier representatives were experts in having a good time, especially after the mission was complete. In fact, that was their main job: to keep their customers *happy*, and they were well qualified to do that. In the course of inspecting the glass being manufactured, we were exposed to the hot end, meaning where the molten glass was transferred from the molds. The temperature is usually over 110 degrees, and you get dehydrated really quick. We left to come back and drove for a couple of hours and stopped at Riney's Bar Club on Walnut Street (now Muhammad Ali Boulevard) and preceded to drink up all their booze. Al was drinking Orange Blossoms (Vodka and orange pulp), and I stuck with whiskey. He was enamored with the woman piano player, so we stayed until midnight because he wasn't used to being rebuked by any female. Most of them fell right into his arms. We must have consumed at least ten drinks apiece and got home about 3:00 a.m. I, of course, went to work the next day. He called me on the phone about noon to see if I came to work and was surprised. He said that when we relieved himself, everything looked orange. I, being half his age, felt bad but otherwise OK. Another memorable episode to write about.

Majestic Prince won the 1969 Kentucky Derby with only eight colts in the race. He was sired by Raise a Native and Native Dancer, two generations back. The small number of horses entered was due to the caliber of good horses in the race. It appeared that it was between four horses and difficult for us to make a choice. Bill Hartack's winning ride aboard Majestic Prince tied him with Eddie Arcaro as one of the two jockeys to win five Kentucky Derbies. Arcaro's record had stood alone for seventeen years. Majestic Prince was one of the most striking animals I had ever seen, and he sparkled like a new penny. Other notable colts in the race were Arts and Letters, Dike, and Top Knight. We bet on Top Knight off his race in the Florida Derby and ignored the advice of my father, who said he had "been in the barn too long," which proved to be correct. He (Top Knight) ran fifth and folded in the stretch run. We lost for the second straight year, but we gulped a few anyway.

Due to a big stake with Proud Clarion (1967), we adopted a new betting strategy that included a small bet to win and our big bet to show, as always. This gave us two horses—one a longshot (> 8–1) to win and cover our bet with our favorite selection to show. This laid the ground for future betting other than the Kentucky Derby. We would have bragging-right bets and moneymaking bets, possibly at the same time. Our ability to read the racing form and determine who were legitimate contenders (without bias) was instrumental in determining our betting and money management.

In 1970, Dust Commander won the Kentucky Derby and paid $32.60 to win on a good track. The weather was a bit chilly but not too uncomfortable. We bet the entry High Echelon and Personality to show and High Echelon came in third and paid $4.40, a good return on investment (ROI). We couldn't pass up betting two horses for the price of one with two excellent well-bred animals. Incidentally, an entry bet was my father's favorite bet, and it served us well over the years. Dust Commander had won the Bluegrass Stakes at Keenland ten days prior, but was overlooked by most experts, so to speak. Ha!

The day before the derby (May 1), of course, was the Kentucky Oaks for fillies. A woman who worked in our lab was going to the Oaks with her soon-to-be husband, and I read the form most of the night and made a selection in each race to assist her in determining what to bet. I gave her $10 to bet all nine of my picks for each race in a show parlay, which means you bet the first horse to show $10 and, if it shows (third), take all of the winning and bet it on the next race to show, so on and so on. Believe it or not, each of the first eight races I picked ran at least third, and by the last race of the day (one after the Oaks), she had accumulated approximately $500. It took up most of their spare time, and her fiancé wasn't too happy at all. So they struggled to decide whether to bet on the last race or not, but they followed my instructions to bet, so they did, and the horse I picked ran fourth, how ironic. So all their work was in vain, and I lost $10. That was the last time I ever asked anyone to do that. It screwed up the whole day, and they were not happy even though I had eight horses to run at least third. I lost it all on the ninth bet. It was a lesson I never forgot.

In 1971, Canonero II won the Kentucky Derby, a Venezuelan colt, and he was a member of the betting field (six), which is determined by the track handicapper and are usually the horses he or she considers to have the least chance of winning. Bob and I were standing in our familiar spot at the entrance to the paddock tunnel when they brought the horse over from the barns to be saddled in the paddock. It so happened that Canonero II stopped right in front of us, and when I saw him, he looked superb, but we didn't think he had a chance against nineteen other horses. Now let me tell you of my favorite story:

At a Little League baseball game, an older woman asked me if I would bet $6 ($2 across the board) on a foreign horse. This was approximately two to three weeks before the derby, so I said I would be glad to put the bet up. As of that time, I knew of no foreign horse that was going to run in the derby. There hadn't been one that I could remember ever running in the derby. In those days, any horse could run in the derby if they paid the nomination entry and the starter fees. She had read in the *National Inquirer* that Jeanne Dixon, a soothsayer mystic who predicted all sorts of happenings, insisted that a foreign horse would win the Kentucky Derby. I disregarded her wants and desires and almost forgot about it because, to me, it was so preposterous that I laughed about it. I guess you know the rest of the story. I bet the horse to show just in case and used the other $4 to make a free bet for us. In other words, I held the bet as a bookie would do. To make a long story short, I had to pay her off out of my pocket, $31.60. I was fortunate enough that he only paid $19.40 to win, $8.00 to place, and $4.20 to show. If he had not been a member of the mutual field (six horses), he would have probably paid over $100 to win. No good deed shall go unpunished.

To back up for a minute, Canonero II was a Venezuelan horse that was shipped to Florida at the last minute to be quarantined for a week before running, which was the rule. When he arrived, I had read that he was underweight and had two teeth removed because of infected gums and sores on his body. They shot him full of antibiotics, and he miraculously blossomed out like a brand-new colt, and they shipped him to Churchill Downs to run in the Derby. He had been, at the time, the only horse that had run the Derby distance and that, plus feeling good from the meds, made the difference.

Chapter 8

In July of 1971, the production group went to Camp Manitucky in Ontario, Canada, for a seminar and awards week. The company owned three small islands near the Winnipeg River, and we got aboard seaplanes (held together by bailing wire) and landed on the main island, which was equipped with a lodge, cabins, a large eatery, and plenty of workers and booze. It had a large cabin cruiser, speedboats, and smaller john boats, etc. There were approximately fifty men that took the trip, and all were expected to give a dissertation on a subject that would be beneficial to the company. I wasn't prepared for how cold it was there, down in the mid-thirty degrees, and I didn't bring adequate clothing. The very first night, Bill and a bunch of younger guys took the speed boat out in the pitch-black darkness. The only light being on the boat. Wild Bill was at the helm and, of course, had the accelerator wide open in strange waters. A recipe for disaster. All, of course, were inebriated and lacked any judgment or sense of moderation. Jim was lying on the bow of the boat, supposedly directing where to go, etc. They avoided a deadly disaster by turning the boat barely away from a sheer cliff wall, and then they crashed into a small reef shortly thereafter. It tore a large hole in the bottom of the boat and propelled Jim some thirty feet onto the rocks. The others almost drowned, and miraculously, none were seriously hurt. A good way to start off a holiday. When they didn't come back, they sent out a search party and fortunately found them in the darkness. The boat was completely demolished. I was ten to fifteen years older than those idiots and was not with them, thank God! Other lesser shenanigans went on constantly as if to see which one would outdo the other, I guess. They had a ping-pong tournament (doubles) the next day, and my partner and I won a prize to be given later. I knew we would win because after I saw who we were up against, it was easy; we just let them make mistakes, and that was that. After all had made their presentations, the next day, we went on a fishing trip with Indian guides. Two of us in small john boats were to compete for the most and largest fish caught. It was so cold (midthirties), and before I left, I had enough sense to go into the towel room and wrap several towels around my body and head and hat, etc. Even with that, I damn near froze to death out on Winnipeg River with the boat engines wide open at full speed. When we met the guides at Minaki, a small village of Indians, we all dashed to obtain the first boat and guide that was available; and everyone grabbed a fifth of whiskey to take along. The company had just acquired a new brand from Canada that was 80° to 86°, and that was what I grabbed to take because that was all that was left. We took off like stripped ass apes led by our guide to his favorite fishing spot. We mostly fished deep for walleyes and northern pike. I drank all but one sip of the 25.6 oz. of whiskey to keep warm and caught no fish. That afternoon, we had a fish fry on the banks of the river, and the weather had warmed up considerably. As we rounded a bend in a small cove, we found another fishing boat with the Indian guide and passengers all passed out from excess alcohol consumption and the boat bobbing in the water. The fish that were caught were cooked right on the spot, and the food was delicious. There were other notorious and nefarious events that occurred during our stay at Manitucky. The next day we had a horseshoe pitching tournament, and I won that also. I was a very good horseshoe pitcher from my early childhood. I had been underpaid and needed any prize I could muster—a toaster and an electric can opener came in handy. Later that day, one of my bosses took Bill and I out on a fishing trip. It had become very warm, and we had a quart of gin to drink as we haphazardly fished. There were numerous little islands that we navigated around, and Bill's fishing line got caught on a rock, and as we continued to troll, he neglected to say anything about it and his line was let out to the max. We had to retrace our route in order to retrieve his fishing line, and we had a big laugh about that. When we returned to the lodge and were eating dinner, we both thought we were having a heat stroke due to the sun and gin we soaked up. We had been cold the previous days, and I had never seen the temperature change so rapidly in a couple of days. The large cabin cruiser had also been grounded in shallow waters and was listing and had to be abandoned. When we left on the seaplane the next day and we passed over the islands, it looked like Pearl Harbor after the Japanese attacked on December 7, 1941. I thought for sure the Production Department would be held responsible, but the company had evidentially experienced similar occurrences in the past from other groups. A designated photographer had been assigned to take various photos of everyone doing various activities, and we all were given a montage of the photos for our keeping. I still have that framed montage and can look back on that time and enjoy the memories.

Also, that year, 1971–1972, the oldest son of the owner's family took over as CEO, and one of his first acts was to raise everyone's pay to equal similar jobs in the surrounding areas for the first time in fifteen years. I received a decent salary that befitted my position. We couldn't believe the surprising turn of events, and I was overjoyed to say the least.

CHAPTER 9

In 1972, Riva Ridge won the Kentucky Derby on a beautiful day, and the weather was ideal and the track was fast. He took the lead from the start and went wire to wire, winning by about four lengths. There were fifteen colts in the race; therefore, the show payoff was good, being he was the favorite at 3–2. He was owned by Meadow Stud (C. T. Chenery) and ridden by R. Turcotte. His sire was First Landing, who was sired by Turn-To, one of my father's old-time favorite bloodlines. This was a slam-dunk bet to show, and we cashed in to some degree even though he paid only $3 to show. Incidentally he was trained by Lucien Laurin, a long-time trainer who was noted for his patience with young horses. We celebrated as usual up until Sunday morning. The ROI of 50 percent can't be passed up if you are looking for a money return, rather than a bragging-rights bet. We, of course, followed our routine of arriving at the track at about 9:00 a.m. in order to obtain a nice spot in the lawn of the paddock with our usual supplies. Food, whiskey, gin, vodka, beer, and few ginger ales to mix with or a jug of lemonade; and we let the good times roll.

In the meantime, we were still betting races at other tracks, mostly on a Saturday, at my father's house and imbibing to our hearts' content. I would get up early on Saturday, and my son Gene and I would go to Steidin's Grocery Store nearby to buy the groceries for the week and do other chores before going to play the horses. Fortunately, my wife, Doris, was busy trying to keep the home fires burning. Most wives would not tolerate my behavior, but she was tolerant of me to the highest degree, or I would have never participated in these types of activities. She (Doris) had gone with us several times, but it wasn't her cup of tea. My mother went off and on when she felt like it and my father wasn't drinking. They knew that we were only interested in the horses, and that was our saving grace as far as they were concerned. Gambling, small time, and at least breaking even were the lesser of nefarious activities that most people who attended the Kentucky Derby went there for, and that was the advantage we had, especially on Derby Day because, as you know, you were playing against the other players and the track (house) was taking a cut from every bet that was made and most of these revelers lost money and didn't seem to care as long as they could dress up and try to impress others. It was like taking candy from a baby. Somebody had to do it! Har har.

It was in the prime of my life, and I never felt better. My feet hardly touched the ground (ha) except every other step. I had no other ambitions except to enjoy myself without hurting others. Most everybody else was scrambling to get ahead (promotion) or pay off their mortgage and other debts, while I was saving my greenbacks and reading racing forms cover to cover. Over the years, I never threw racing forms, tickets, or programs away and kept them for posterity. The reason I kept the forms was to study them later on as to what clues I could ascertain from those horses who had won the day before. Believe me, it paid off in spades. Others were preoccupied with their own idiosyncrasies like keeping up with the Joneses and living beyond their means. I never cared about the Joneses, and as far as I was concerned, that was a foolish endeavor and I was not a social climber. Also, my father, Bob, and I purchased a small amount of company stock when it was selling lower than usual. I held mine for the next fifty years, and guess what?

Meanwhile, leadership changed hands in the production area as well as other areas and almost all became toadies, lackies, and yes-men. As usual, no one in the production area got promoted unless they were some kind of engineer. The biggest break I ever had was when they chose a chemical engineer to be the assistant bottling manager, and I understood that I was a candidate. They were probably correct in that decision because dealing with all of the union workers, etc., was a living nightmare, and I wasn't the type of personality to deal with that wishy-washy, tell-me-your-troubles kind of job. Thank God for that break.

I continued to drink and smoke on my leisure time. I never drank while I was working because I didn't have time, because I was literally running a one-man show (one other half-assed person to help inspect incoming materials). I now had the mental and physical wherewithal to withstand the weird decisions that the ship of fools was floating on. With the top brand that the company purchased in 1958, not even the gross incompetence could stop the juggernaut that accounted for 90 percent of the profit that the company produced. So on we sailed into the unknown, and I lived where I always had, while others lived beyond their means to impress others and satisfy their unwarranted egos!

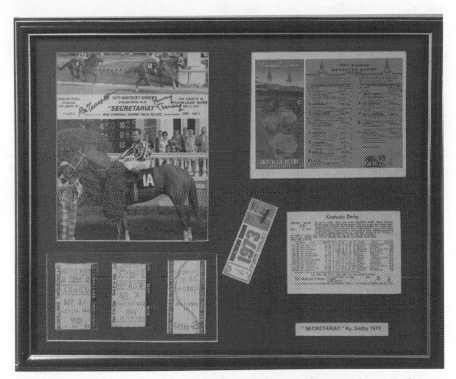

$2 Winning Tickets for all three Triple Crown Races; winner circle photo signed; Derby Program; Newspaper Race Chart & Ticket

The great Secretariat won the Kentucky Derby on May 5, 1973, in record time of 1:59 2/5 for the 1 ¼ miles. The weather was a bit chilly, but couldn't have been better by race time. The first time ever under two minutes. He also was owned by the estate of C. T. Chenery and trained by Lucien Laurin, the previous winners from the year before. Bill, the packaging manager, and I had become good friends; and he went with us to the derby to have some fun. Secretariat ran third in the Wood Memorial in New York (prep race), where his stable mate, Angel Light, won. Lucien did not extend Secretariat in order to save him for the derby as a fresh horse. He had won most of his races as a two-year-old and was already looked upon as a super horse. He was by Bold Ruler/Somethingroyal, the daughter of Princequillo blood on the distaff and looked superb in the paddock. There also was another very good colt in the race by the name of Sham, who had blitzed everyone in California and won the Santa Anita Derby in a cake walk. We knew it was between these two colts, and we bet Sham to show, and he paid $3. it was kind of a disappointment, but we won nevertheless. Incidentally, Sham also broke the existing derby track record while running second, two lengths behind Secretariat. The CD track was made lightning fast that day to accommodate a potential record. The only time Secretariat ran out of the money was on the first start, which he ran fourth. He was, and is, considered to be one of the best three horses of the twentieth century. The other two being Man O' War in the 1920s and Citation of the late 1940s. My father, who saw all of them, maintained that Man O' War was the greatest of them all even though he did not run in the Kentucky Derby.

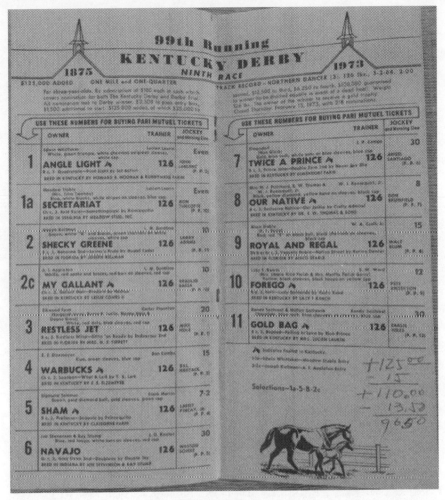

1973 – Kentucky Derby Program

My father took it upon himself to write a small booklet in 1971 on thoroughbred race horses called *Guidelines for Players of the Thoroughbreds* and dedicated it to the memory of his father, Gene Sutton, who liked to talk of his experiences in handling horses for more than fifty years, which rubbed off on him. Francis Eugene Sutton, my grandfather, was a blacksmith and later a carriage house owner. We had finally determined, after years of research and betting, the only way to bet on regular races, other than the Kentucky Derby, was to bet our #1 selection to place and a longshot contender to win. This was to minimize your losses. A very conservative way of betting. He and I arrived at that conclusion after many years of research revealed this option. You had a chance of collecting on both bets and saving your money you bet on the other hand. It payed off very well until the exotics betting became a betting choice later on. His booklet is available through my family if wanted. A very simple solution to a complicated subject with numerous variables to contend with. I assisted him to some degree in this endeavor.

In the meantime, we had been traveling to Keenland Race Track some seventy-five miles away for weekends when they were running, always right before CD opened its spring and fall meets. This was a beautiful track in the countryside, and in those days of the '70s to '80s, the horses were easy to pick; and most of the time, we won because of the big difference between the circuit horses, Fairgrounds and at Florida tracks, etc., and the big horse farms in the Lexington area was different and the local owners mostly had top-bred fresh horses to run. We would have five to six winners a day and always had a great time going up (sipping) and coming home (gulping), always stopping for more booze and Rebecca Ruth bourbon balls for my mother. This was before the interstate was built and we took the two-lane highways. This was prior to the '70s.

The one hundredth Kentucky Derby was won by Cannonade on May 4, 1974, and the weather was chilly but satisfactory, and the track was fast. The derby in 1974 had the largest crowd to ever see the Kentucky Derby, where 164,000 attended. He was sired by Bold Bidder (Bold Ruler) out of a Ribot mare (Queen Sucree) and trained by the great Woody Stephens, who later won five consecutive Belmont stakes, a record that still stands today. Cannonade was in an entry, and we couldn't pass up betting it even though it only paid $2.40 to show. Our win bet choice was Little Current, who was 22–1. He was owned by Darby Dan Farm, the same owners that had Proud Clarion in 1967. We thought we had another high-odds winner. He might have won but got blocked by others in the far turn and closed very well. He later won the Preakness two weeks later. If (big word) he had not been interfered with, we would have still been celebrating. A turn of bad luck for us, but that's part of horse racing. Saving winning $2 tickets had become a collection item, and we bet $2 on every horse in the one hundredth derby race to make sure we had a winning ticket for posterity. We did this for both Secretariat and Cannonade because of the likelihood of them winning. Bill and I saved all the losing tickets also, besides the daily racing forms and program, which are part of my Kentucky Derby memorabilia. This foresight became <u>invaluable</u> in the years to come. Bob Wolf, my friend, became less interested even though he accompanied us on Derby Day. He had three daughters who were attending Catholic schools, and his funds were becoming limited and his frugality prevented him from making any large bets. He saved a lot of greenbacks this way; but Bob, Bill, and myself all could analyze the past performances (PPs) very well. Bob, from the early days with my father, and I, and later Bill, learned how to read the DRF very quickly and played devil's advocate with each other to seek out a winner. We all spent very little or nothing for refreshments at the concession stands, because they were too pricey and we had our own booze and only needed ice, if we could find it. We might buy a large cup of ice, but no soft drinks or beer—too expensive, even though we were betting our money on the iffy proposition of gambling.

By the way my oldest son, Francis Eugene, met with an unfortunate accident when he was sixteen that ended his athletic aspirations. He was playing a pick up game of basketball at his high school on Sunday when we was undercut while he was shooting a jump shot. He suffered a spiral compound break of his tibia and fibula and was in a full leg cast and was on crutches for at least eight months. Another unfortunate incident that had to be dealt with accordingly.

Foolish Pleasure won the 1975 Kentucky Derby on a drizzly, cloudy day, and the track was listed as fast. The grand sire was Bold Ruler out of a Tom Fool mare, and he had won the Hopeful and Champagne as a two-year-old. It was an easy pick to show, and he paid $3.60 to show, a nice return. However, we bet the Prince Thou Art entry to win and show, and he ran sixth; what I thought was a good bet turned out to be a fluke. I liked it because he was owned by

Darby Dan Farms, which treated us good in the past. My buddy Bill called him Prince Thou Ain't. I was disappointed in my selection and realized I let bias influence my decision. Since we had bet most of our money on the Prince, we needed a winner in the last race to at least salvage something. It started raining hard, and we were huddled under the stands, and the track turned sloppy. Bob picked a horse from Hazel Park named Sketchmaker at 10–1 odds, and we bet our last dollars on him to win. We, in desperation, bet $50 on him, and he won by a nose in the last jump. We were beyond elated and really got <u>smashed</u> after that good fortune, and we broke even for the day. A truly one-time event for us.

About this time, '75 to '76, exotic betting started in most of the race tracks, and Bill and I saw this as an opportunity to cash in. Ha ha. Since we had been so successful in our simple strategy, of a value bet of > 8–1 to win and the favorite or our first choice to place, we deduced that a trifecta would be easy since a #2 trifecta box only cost $12, we couldn't lose much. In any event, we decided to travel to Florida for the Flamingo. We holed up in a nice hotel and went to the track for two days and studied the racing form until our eyes popped out. Hialeah Race Track was the most beautiful track I had ever seen, and the first day, we won substantially and were elated and took pictures of each other surrounded by $100 bills. We drank a little more than our regular pint of whiskey.

We went to the track early on Saturday to enjoy the surroundings, and the weather was absolutely beautiful. We broke about even on the races leading up to the Flamingo. However, before the races started at about 10:00 a.m., we saw Jim McKay come out of the broadcast trailer and went over to take some photos and talk with him. We still have the photos of our off-chance meeting. Howard Cosell was in the trailer but wouldn't come out because he didn't have his toupee on yet (snicker). We went down there to bet Honest Pleasure, who was the heavy favorite, and we bet our stash on him to show and made only a couple hundred bucks, but all in all, we paid for our trip. We vowed we would come back to this beautiful track, which was not situated in the best part of town.

Bold Forbes won the 1976 Kentucky Derby, on a cool cloudy day on May 1, 1976. He was grand-sired by Bold Ruler and had excellent bloodlines on the distaff and was ridden by Angel Cordero Jr., a hot jockey at the time. We, however, were so enamored by Honest Pleasure that we bet him to win and heavy to show. He only paid $2.20 to show because there were only nine horses in the race, and Honest Pleasure was bet down to 0.40 on the dollar (2–5 odds). We broke even for the day and consumed our usual ration of booze to ward off the boogeyman. My father would not bet the derby because he would not bet on an odds-on favorite (less than even money).

Each year since about 1958, we went to Keeneland for the Bluegrass Stakes, which later became an important prep for the derby; and we only missed one up to this point. As I stated previously, it was a picturesque setting but did not have a race-caller, so you had to be on your toes to know when post time was or you could not bet. Bill had joined Bob and me for those sessions. We drank beer on the way there, whiskey while we were there, and both on the way back. Fortunately for us, drunk-driving laws were not as stringent as they are now or we would still be in jail.

Most of the beverages we consumed were either purchased, furnished by our vendors, tourist samples, or later reimbursed by the company from purchased receipts that were allocated to the workers depending on their positions. (all tax paid)

1977 Program – Seattle Slew – signed by winning Jockey – Jean Cruguet

$2 Win Tickets for all three Triple Crown Races;
Winners Circle photo for Seattle Slew & corresponding Programs

On May 7, 1977, Seattle Slew won the Kentucky Derby, and the weather was cloudy with the temperature in the seventies and the track was fast. I went to the track on a bus with my second cousin because Bob and Bill weren't available. I had been saving my shekels for some time, waiting for an ideal opportunity to find a colt that I firmly believed in. I bet $2,200 on Seattle Slew to <u>show</u>, and he paid $2.80 to show. Before I went to the window, my cousin grabbed $100 bill from my hands to bet on whatever. This was the largest amount of money I have ever bet on any race to date. I won about $900 that day, and I was elated. My cousin expected me to give him a cut, but I told him he already took his out. We finally got home about 9:00 p.m. on the bus. His bloodlines were impeccable with Bold Ruler and Hail to Reason, three back and Round Table on the bottom side. He broke from the gate clumsily and almost lost it, but he recovered quickly and bullied his way up to second by the clubhouse turn and stayed there all the way and took command at the 3/8ths pole and went on to win. I took a big chance that day, which was unlike me, and it worked out. Seattle Slew went on to win the Triple Crown and proved to be one of the ten best horses of the twentieth century. He was ridden by Jean Cruguet and owned by Karen Taylor and trained by William Turner Jr.

For the last five years, we had been going to Keeneland as guests of our vendors. Bill C. was the gentleman that belonged to the Keeneland Club, an exclusive club reserved for owners and big bettors, and we went to the dining room right above the paddock so we could see the horses being saddled. It was an ideal situation, and we had many pleasant times there, with lunch, valet parking, and all the booze we could consume. They were memorable times that I shall never forget, and Mr. Bill C., a World War II prisoner of war, was the perfect host. We went from tuna fish and bologna sandwiches in the '50s and '60s to fine dining. It was some of the best times of my life. All Bill and I had to do was pick the horses to bet on, and that was our MO anyway. We had good times going with two six packs of beer to consume on the way and talk, etc. Usually four of us, several high balls before lunch and during the races. On the way home (seventy-five miles), we drank liberally from the whiskey we brought with us. It tested our alcohol consumption quantity, but all were confirmed drinkers and were used to hangovers.

By now we were establishing a tradition of attending the Bluegrass Stakes on the Thursday (ten days) before the derby. Another vendor played host, and we went to the backside (barn) down Rice Road, which led to the entrance of the barns and before you arrived at the main gate. Another vendors rep, Bill H. took coolers of drinks and sandwiches to eat picnic style in the beautiful country setting of the area, and almost always the weather was good. Our entourage grew until we had several cars and ten to twelve people participating, and it didn't cost us a dime. Because of our positions in the company, as far as purchasing and bottling supplies, the vendors were more than happy to make us happy.

In late April of 1978, this same group traveled to Keeneland for the Bluegrass Stakes and settled in on the back side to picnic before the races started. We naturally had plenty of food and drinks, and the weather was ideal. We all looked forward to seeing Alydar, the great Calumet colt who had sparked the imagination of horsemen around the country. This colt was about the end of the line for the Calumet dynasty, and no one in our group was going to bet against him. It was one of the cases where it was foolish to bet at all, but we all agreed that we would pool our resources and bet him to win for the sake of bragging rights in the years to come.

I was elected to make the bet. Keeneland had a room where they had $100 windows to bet in. As you probably know, they still had the old cardboard stiff pari-mutuel tickets that had to be punched by the teller one at a time, and it was time consuming to say the least. They had about ten to fifteen lines (windows) to bet in, and when I got in the back of one of the lines, I thought that I would never get the bets up. I had approximately $2,500 to bet to win, the largest bet I was ever going to make. In front of two lines were two men with suitcases of money to bet, and one bet $35,000 and the other $50,000. Those lines did not move at all because every $100 ticket had to be punched. They just held their finger down on the button, and the tickets spewed out one by one. I was in another line, and I didn't think I would get the bet placed by post time. A man behind me asked if he could go ahead of me to get his bets up. I said absolutely not, and he got pissed off. What a shame! In any event, I did actually get the bet placed as the bell rang to close the window, which had stayed open because the track delayed post time so most could get their bets placed, much to their dismay, because all the betting on one horse created a minus pool even with the track only paying 5¢ on the dollar and the track lost money on that race because they had to pay the minimum. This was the only time in my lifetime to date that I ever saw that much money bet on one horse, and doubt I will ever see it again.

At the time Churchill Downs didn't even have any $100 windows on the ground floor. Alydar won, of course, and we split up the proceeds of $125, and all were happy, which amounted to about $20 each. A once-in-a-lifetime experience.

Affirmed won the 1978 Kentucky Derby and was ridden by Steve Cauthen a seventeen-year-old phenom from Kentucky on a pleasant day and a fast track. He beat the big horse Alydar in a duel down to the wire. Affirmed had also beaten about all other horses in races that Alydar had not been entered, which made for a much-anticipated derby matchup. Both were bet down to low odds, and the payouts were slim. We, of course, bet Alydar to show and won a few dollars; he paid $2.40 to show, and Affirmed paid $2.60 to show and $5.60 to win. This was the beginning of the great rivalry between the colts. Affirmed went on to win the Triple Crown and beat Alydar by the slightest of margins each time and was one of the greatest rivalries of all time. Both horses were Hall-of-Famers and gave the horse racing industry nationwide notoriety.

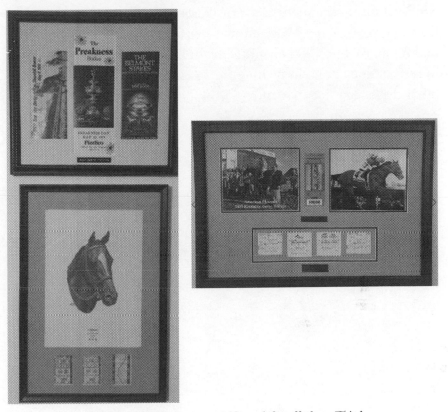

$2 Winning Tickets on Affirmed for all three Triple
Crown Races and corresponding Programs

Spectacular Bid won the 1979 Kentucky Derby and was the odds-on favorite at 3–5 on a chilly day on a fast track. He was trained by Bud Delp, a rather eccentric braggart and ridden by R. Franklin, an unknown jockey at the time. He was sired by Bold Bidder (by Bold Ruler) again and won easily. He was a gray colt and looked superb in the paddock. He had won seven races as a two-year-old and was already deemed to be the best at the time. He paid $2.80 to show and we won again, but not that much. He was a standout in the racing form and was a slam-dunk bet. He had won the Bluegrass Stakes at Keeneland, the Flamingo, and the Florida Derby previously. He appeared to be another Triple Crown but ran third in the Belmont Stakes. He was out of the money only one time when he finished fourth. He won twenty-six out of thirty races in his three-year career. We again had our Keeneland back-side party and regular Churchill Downs picnic in front of the large tote board in the paddock area. I saw him up close and personal as I had seen all of the others since 1940.

CHAPTER 10

Tom Sutton - 18 years old - Pre accident

In 1978, another tragedy confronted our family. My youngest son Thomas, who was nineteen years old went on a weekend trip to Otter Creek Park with three other guys. This park is situated on a bluff overlooking the Ohio River in Meade County, Kentucky, about forty miles south of Louisville. It had cabins and rustic trails, etc.

While horsing around with his buddies, he ran down a decline for some unknown reason and didn't realize that a three-hundred-foot cliff lay beyond that was hidden by the tall trees growing out of the outcroppings, disguising the drop-off. Before he could stop himself, he tried to catch on to a tree trunk, and it spun him around and over the edge. All two hundred pounds of him hit a ledge about fifteen feet down and continued to bounce off trees and out cropping of rocks until he lay unconscious three hundred feet below near the railroad track that ran along the river's edge. The authorities took some time before they were able to locate him due to the rough terrain. They carried him out on a stretcher, and believe it or not, he was still breathing. They ambulanced him to Saints Mary and Elizabeth Hospital in Louisville and notified us. The other three boys witnessed the fall, and they told us about it later. He had a severe skull fracture, a broken shoulder, broken ribs, and cracked vertebrae, and was in a coma for three weeks, alternating between life and death. When he finally woke up, he was helpless and couldn't talk, walk, eat, etc. They had to perform a tracheotomy to keep him alive. His brain stem has been severely injured, and I believe that not for the grace of God and his superior physical condition, he would have passed away. He was a wrestler in high school, and he worked out with weights and all kinds of exercise programs, and he was in the prime of his life. Super strong and healthy. I believe that he thought he was bulletproof, just as I had also falsely believed, which was par for the course for a young man, especially of his nature. We took turns watching over him while in the hospital for another month while they tried to rehabilitate him. He could not even sit up and did not remember who we were or anything. The neurosurgeon, Dr. Sexton, said his brain stem had been permanently damaged, and his recovery was doubtful. To have survived this fall was a miracle in and of itself. My wife and I agreed that she would attend to his emotional needs while I would attend to his physical rehabilitation. To this day, forty years later, these emotional needs are constant, and she has faithfully stood by his side to help him in every way. He has no memory of the accident and hardly any short-term memory at all. My wife and daughter (Debbie) are the caretakers for him even though he lives in an apartment complex by himself. My job was easier because he slowly partially regained his motor skills and took long walks of five miles or more every day. That was the key to his physical recovery for ten years. The accident and recovery was so spectacular that the newspaper (the *Courier Journal*) published two articles on the incident. My accident when I was fourteen, as previously stated, and now his accident made me wonder if we were destined to suffer because of an inherent aggressive attitude that led to hardships and then test our mettle to carry on under adverse circumstances.

Genuine Risk won the 1980 Kentucky Derby on a clear day on a fast track. She was only the second filly to win the Kentucky Derby; the other was the great Regret in 1915. She was a Native Dancer offspring four back and had a good turn of foot. She paid $28.60 to win and was a surprise to us. She went on to run second in the Preakness and Belmont Stakes. She had run third in the Wood Memorial right before the derby and was primed very well by the trainer Leroy Jolley. We bet Plugged Nickle, who ran seventh and lost all the way around, but we were not deterred in our ability to celebrate our loss.

Early in 1981, Bill and I went to Hialeah again and this time met we met my old boss, Lee, who hired me in 1956 and later left to work for Pratt and Whitney in Florida. There were no particular standouts that year in the Flamingo. We just had a grand time and enjoyed the beautiful weather and broke about even at the track. For a change, nothing noteworthy occurred, but we did have our moments and bought some hats and other souvenirs. We still have the Hialeah sun visors and still wear them occasionally.

Later that year, we took a purchasing junket with our label supplier to go fishing off the coast of New Jersey for bluefish, etc. We went out early on the boat named *Apple Jack* after that mild alcoholic drink. There were five of us besides the pilot on this great fishing boat. They furnished the fishing equipment, bait, and everything else. We each took turns sitting in the fishing line seat and fishing belts that was available. With plenty to drink, the captain led us right onto the heart of the bluefish school, and we caught about twenty-five—they were ten to fifteen pounds each. We had a grand time without going into further detail. They asked if we wanted the fish we caught sent back to Louisville, and I said I would take them. About a week later, a large crate of fish turned up at the airport all iced down, and they called me up and told me to come out and pick them up; they didn't want any part of that crate. I went out and could barely lift the crate into my trunk with water dripping from the package. I tried to eat one, but they were too gamey and not very tasty. I called Bob, my frugal buddy, to see if he wanted them. He picked them up the same day and took them to eat. He soaked them in milk, and it took some of the gaminess away, and they eventually ate them all. I didn't know what I would have done with them if he had not taken them. This trip was one of the most memorable ones we ever took, and we still laugh about it today.

The next day, we went to the Monmouth Race Track originally to make a little money. We lost most of our money on a horse that I picked, and we bet it to win and it placed. Another lesson long forgotten from by-gone days.

We didn't have any transportation, and the last bus leaving the track didn't want to let us on because they were full, but we paid the driver extra and he let us on. The supplier who had sponsored this trip had an emergency and had to fly home prior to our Monmouth visit, so we were short of funds. On the bus, we had no idea where we were or where we were going. Bill and his boss went to the back of the bus, and I sat next to a Puerto Rican named Johnny in the middle of the bus. They were all smoking weed in the back, and the whole bus was filled with smoke. We were passing through an abandoned and run-down section of Monmouth, New Jersey, and it occurred to me that we might be in a world of hurt. I asked Johnny where we should disembark. The people in the back told us to get off at the next stop, but Johnny told me not to do that because we would be robbed or beaten. So I told my buddies, and we got off the bus further down the road. When we left the bus, we were in a desolate, deserted rail road track and warehouses area, and the only humans that were there were four unsavory characters standing in front of the rail road station twirling chains attached to their belts and one old auto sitting off to the side. We made a beeline for the car, which was used as a taxi cab, with the driver asleep in the front seat. We asked him he would take us to a hotel, and he said *yes*. Thank God! Bill and I jumped in the back seat piled with dirty clothes and half eaten cans of pork and beans. He obviously lived in his car. He took us downtown, and we paid him as much as we could spare. We had return plane tickets already, but not enough money to eat breakfast. So here we are, three broke executives wondering how we let ourselves get into this kind of predicament. We made it back, of course, but the whole trip was an experience we would never forget, and we laugh about it now and tell the same story over and over when we get together (two of us now). You're never too old to make a mistake, so we returned on another fishing trip to New Jersey with a different supplier in 1982 and went to Saratoga Race Track in upstate New York. More on that later on.

In 1981, Pleasant Colony won the Kentucky Derby on a clear and chilly day and paid $9.00 to win and $4.40 to show. He was ridden by Jorge Velazquez, who later became a leading jockey. There were twenty-one colts entered, and that's why the payoffs were above average. Pleasant Colony was out of Ribot (two back) and a Double Jay mare (four back generations). He was our pick, and we also bet Woodchopper, the horse who ran second that paid $23.40 to place and $13.00 to show. We noticed that Woodchipper had a 1':38" mile workout four days before the derby, and I had never seen that before, so we took a chance on him to place. Needless to say, we were overjoyed and had a few extra shots of heart medicine to celebrate. Oh happy days! Pleasant Colony had won the Wood Memorial three weeks before and looked spectacular in the paddock. He later also won the Preakness and Travers and was third in the Belmont Stakes and was a prolific sire.

In the meanwhile, we made our trip to Keeneland for the Bluegrass Stakes in April between 1974 and 1981 and picnicked at the back and then staggered over to the track to do our serious drinking and betting. These were some of the most memorable times of my life, and to tell the whole story would take another treatise.

Gato Del Sol won the 1982 Kentucky Derby with nice weather on a fast track and surprised all of the experts and paid $44.40 to win. He was ridden by Eddie Delahoussaye. He had run second in the Bluegrass Stakes ten days prior, and we overlooked him completely. My friend Jim was the only one that bet on him and cashed in handsomely. We went to the derby with our major supplier of glass bottles and that consisted of a three-day party consisting of dining, golfing, two days at the race track, and every amenity that anyone would want. They had three derby boxes for their guests that held six seats each. We had eight couples from our company and the rest from other customers, plus their personnel. Since I had become assistant purchasing director, Doris and I were now yearly invites to this blowout weekend. We bet El Baba, who ran eleventh—the worst showing of my career. The winner went from starting last to ending first and won easily. However, the whole weekend was outstanding. My problem was very little shut-eye because on Thursday and Friday nights after exhausting socializing, etc., I had to go home and study the racing form for the next day. So I got about three or four hours of sleep two nights in a row and was pooped out.

The supplier regional manager retired (Joe), and Dick S. replaced him and was a gracious host to all. Since I went from sitting on the tote board lawn to great box seats, my wife, Doris, also now accompanied me, and it cost me at least $1,000 for new clothes, etc. What a bummer, but she thoroughly enjoyed the attention and ambiance of the gala experience, and this went on for the next ten years.

Later that year, we went to Point Pleasant, New Jersey, for another fishing trip with a couple of vendors (expenses paid) and then went on to Saratoga Race Track, one of the oldest and prestigious tracks in the country. It still is a summer vacation spot for the rich and famous because back in the nineteenth century, there was a spa that people went for health reasons.

Sunny's Halo won the 1983 Kentucky Derby; the weather was threatening all day, but the track was fast, and there were twenty colts in the race. He was ridden by Eddie Delahoussaye and paid $7 to win. We bet the A entry to show, and they ran fifth and ninth respectively. We lost on the Derby, but broke even for the rest of the day. Since I was the so-called expert among the eighteen people in the three boxes, I was chosen to pick and bet the show parlay where each person or couple could put in $10, and the pot was bet on a horse to show in each race. We had built up a considerable pot, and I bet it all on the Derby and we lost. Needless to say, I wasn't very popular the rest of the day and night.

Churchill Downs – Odds (Totalizer) Board – Circa 1983

Later that year, we took another fishing trip sponsored by our label supplier to Lakeland, Florida. This was a unique place to fish. Our suppliers' ink vendor owned the land that was now an old phosphate mine that had been abandoned for years and became a maze of waterways and channels that no one was allowed into except the caretaker. He was a young (twenty-five) country boy who was the guardian of the place. We met him early in the morning, and he had all the equipment we needed, especially a big cooler of beer. We had no idea what we were about to experience. Once we arrived at the spot and started to put the boat into the water, we heard this loud low roar. Lamar, the guide, told us it was a bull alligator that heard us and was expressing his anger as to our entrance into his domain. Lamar was the only person allowed into the area, and he had marked his route with white pieces of cloth to show him the way in and out of the most eerie prehistoric places I have ever seen; we didn't know such a place existed. It was something to see and experience with its moss-covered trees, winding channels, many water birds, and alligators galore. We had two john boats with outboard motors and trolling motors, plus a case of beer for each boat. Bill and I were with Lamar, and he was a good ole boy who probably considered us city slickers, and he was right!

Believe me when I tell you that the silence was deafening, except for our motors, which were running softly. The whole scene was a primeval scene like out of a movie, and it gave you an uneasy feeling. Lamar told us to be very quiet, and he turned the motor off after we had fished for a while in order to sneak up on "the king of the swamp" alligator. We had caught fish and stopped to eat a bologna sandwich on a small land mound infested with snakes. After eating, we all climbed back into his boat to see if we could find the king sunbathing on his favorite spot where Lamar knew that he hung out. There were six of us in this small boat, and the water level was about an inch from the top of the boat, and he told us not to move about or we would capsize. The proverbial "don't rock the boat" quote was also true in this circumstance. He trolled very quietly around one of the many bends to try to sneak up on the king, and lo and behold, about one hundred yards away, lay this huge alligator sunning himself on the bank. It was the largest alligator I had ever seen, and it appeared to be about twelve feet long with a huge head. All of us were astonished as to what we were seeing. One of the guys in the boat stood up to take a photo, and the water lapped into the boat. I thought we were going to capsize. I took a photograph of the gator, and I still have it in my album. About that time, a huge white crane landed in a tree right above this gator. He unloaded a white stream of bird crap that landed right on the gator. He looked like he had been white washed. Intentionally, I think so, but the gator slid right into the water in our direction. All of us were petrified with fear that with one swipe of his tail, he would sink the boat and we would be gator meat. I figured he weighed about a thousand pounds and he was furious at being disturbed. Fortunately, we did not lay eyes on him again that day. We went back to fishing in each boat, and lo and behold, Bill and I had another surprise coming. As we rounded a bend (that's all there was, bend after bend), Lamar saw an array of birds (waterfowl, such as cormorants, ducks, geese, and others) all congregated in one spot on the water. They must have found a good fishing spot, and he gunned the motor wide open and headed straight into the middle of this gaggle of large birds. Of course, Bill and I were taken by surprise, and before we knew it, we were being hit by flapping wings and feet and tried to duck and put our arms up to protect ourselves. He damn near scared the bejabbers out of us, and he got a big kick seeing us city slickers trying to avoid the planned melee. What an experience that was, and I can still see that gator and these birds to this very day, thirty-seven years later. We've told this story to all our friends and neighbors, and I could tell that they did not believe us to a degree. They thought we were exaggerating because there are no words in my vocabulary to describe this adventure. I didn't know a place like this in the middle of Florida existed. Lamar was the only one allowed on the property, and we were lucky enough to see and experience a thrill of a lifetime. Incidentally, we drank all of the beer, but we were all sober by the time we got back to shore. We tried to schedule a return trip, but I think the State Department made it a wildlife refuge, and that ended anyone from entering.

Instead, our supplier arranged a trip to Kissimmee, Florida, in 1985 with three or four big lakes in that area. There were about ten or fifteen people on the junket with members of our acquisition the company had made in 1985 and others more recently. We all hired guides to go on this big bass fishing expedition and stayed in a large lodge that accompanied all of us. This was three of us to a speedboat. The guide (his boat), Bill, and myself were in one of the boats. This was two days of fishing with large shiners (small bait fish). The first day out, we caught some medium-sized bass, and believe it or not, the line the guide tied our catch in the water alongside the boat must have broken, and we lost them all on the return to home base. I had hooked a large bass and, being an amateur fisherman, tried to muscle it in, and the damn fishing pole broke in two and I lost it. The guide was not happy with me and told me so. I accepted criticism and went on from there. Most of us drank as much as we could keep down that night and had a good time all around.

We got up around 5:00 a.m. the next morning to go to another lake nearby with a goal of catching some big record bass. First, we stopped by and picked up the bait and arrived at our destinations about thirty minutes later. Our guide had an older boat, and it a lot of sand embedded in the floor covering. As you probably know, they always travel as fast as the boat would go (60 mph or so), and Bill and I were sitting in the rear. All that sand was hitting us in the face as the wind blew it, and we had to cover up to keep from hurting. I think the guides do it on purpose to expose us amateurs to real professionals and get a big kick out of it. We arrived at his favorite location and began to fish. Bill caught a huge bass, about 10.5 pounds, and he was satisfied; however, I was I was unable to catch one before lunch. Later that afternoon, I finally caught a large bass, about 9.5 pounds, and we were all satisfied. The whole group caught a big mess of fish, and we had a big fish fry that night—and they were delicious—as we all exchanged stories. The guide kept telling me to keep my pole up for two days, and we all got a big laugh out of that for the next five years. Bill and I both had our large bass mounted, and I still have mine hanging on the wall with all my Kentucky Derby memorabilia for all to see.

To satisfy all our vendors, I was hard put to accept all their perks, and now that I had been promoted to vice president director of purchasing, I had to refuse going to lunch most of the time and other offers that presented itself. I was hard put to even keep up with all the invitations that came my way. It's a good thing that I had plenty of hard drinking behind me, plus my inherited constitution, or I would not have been able to handle that job and be effective.

I'm only writing about some of the most memorable excursions of my tenure as director. I have many more incredible stories to tell later on about some of them.

The ironic thing about all this was that I really didn't care about all this attention, whereas most people would have welcomed those opportunities. It was almost unbelievable for me, of all people, to be the recipient of all this attention. I still can't believe it! That is one reason that my life was unique and almost like a fairy tale. I went from a mostly forgotten silent kid to this patronizing status. More on that later.

CHAPTER 11

In a synopsis of the contents of this anthology, it is evident that I am stating my accomplishments rather than shortcomings. And I am sure there are those that have experienced more difficult and trying incidents, including those severely injured in fighting wars, etc., and the mentally and physical handicapped; but this account of my life is secondary to those that have endured these fates.

For those of you that lived with despair and disappointment, my point here is that you can't be counted out, and you must build brick by brick, one day at a time, to overcome whatever mill-stone that hangs around your neck; and you must develop an attitude to do it yourself and then others may help you reach your goal. Set you goals high, but not impossible. Start with small goals and build on to the next one, and so on.

Everyone has their own tale to tell, and I have kept silent about what I know for ninety years. If not now, then when? As my mother often said, "There is a time and place to use the power God has given you." Now is the *time* for me. Otherwise, when I pass on, all my knowledge about life will be lost in the dusty archives of history. It is important to me that my descendants are aware of what can be done by focusing and having a purpose. "A journey of 1,000 miles begins with a single step." It is never too late to start. Quit bad habits, such as drinking excessively, smoking, or whatever is preventing you from being what you want to be or become; and leave a positive legacy behind for those of your clan to remember you by, rather than being just another name lost over the eons. The very thing that I never thought of is what has given me this platform and what makes

me unique is the fact that I am the only person on this planet, past
or present, to have attended the iconic Kentucky Derby for eighty-
two years, which was never intended until I suddenly realized the
significance of it when I was seventy years old. And you can take
that to the bank. The toxic soup of nastiness and hate that spews
forth from the internet and their conspiracy theories that no one of
sound mind would or could believe, is mind boggling. It only tends
to substantiate the hidden agendas that I have heretofore mentioned.
Maybe some don't want to know the truth, but the shadow knows
and I know. A day of reckoning is on the horizon for them, and they
know who they are!

The difference between my generation and today's generation
is my generation and those before me did not broadcast their
accomplishments, and if they did, they were criticized. Today, with
the internet available, most people are on Facebook, Twitter, YouTube,
IG, TikTok, etc., sounding off about themselves and speaking their
minds on any subject whether they know anything about it or not.

Since I am ninety years young, I now have decided to join the
me-me generation and keep up with the times, although I do not
use any form of media except to express my opinion in writing this
treatise, and the eighty-two years of Kentucky Derby attendance
has given me a platform to sound off. I didn't even consider it until
I realized that I had attended the derby for seventy-five years and
NBC interviewed me and all the memorabilia that I have saved
and accumulated over this time period to prove it. My turn is now!
If I could have written this ten years ago; it would have been much
easier. I rode the tailwinds of my father, John S. Sutton Sr., and
my grandfather, Francis Eugene Sutton. Without them, none of my
horse racing acumen and Kentucky Derby enthusiasm would have
been possible. What was a hardship for many was routine for me,
and that characteristic, perseverance, and altruistic attitude is what
helped make me distinctly unique; however, my attendance of the
Kentucky Derby is what made me one of a kind. I tested the limits
of human endurance to achieve this accomplishment. The hidden
psyche of self-preservation makes everyone thinks they are the best

in one way or the other—the best vehicle driver, the best lover, the best personality, or the best liar (Trump). I feel like I've disappointed many people in this regard of throwing a monkey wrench into their fantasies, and I feel that it is my duty to expose these hidden agendas, especially when I was young.

My mind has been trained to handle chaos since I was a small boy, and oh! What a blessing that has been. I can name many instances that occurred when I saved the day due to my clalm assessment of the situation.

CHAPTER 12

In 1969, our CEO passed away from a heart attack, and his brother took over even though he was a sick man too. Eventually, our production head took over as CEO, and then we had another engineer take over production. A whole new era was taking place, and we had many changes in personnel. Also new equipment was purchased to speed up the production efficiency, and the whole set up was changed. Before the change, the production efficiency was between 80 percent and 85 percent. After the new machines were installed, it dropped off significantly, something that I never understood. All the people running the show were engineers, as usual. Seemed to me that was a bit odd, but whatever. It didn't affect me in any way, and I went about doing my job as always. I understood later that I has been considered for assistant manager of bottling but wasn't chosen. This was a <u>godsend</u> for me because that job entailed interacting with all the hourly employees, which was a nightmare, and my mindset was indifferent and not suited for employee relations. I was thankful for the piece of luck because I probably would have moved on because it was out of my wheelhouse. A good friend of mine took the job, and it took a toll on him over the years.

In February of 1968, a new packaging assistant was hired named Bill, who later became a dear friend of fifty years and counting. Since our jobs interacted, we worked together at times. Later, he was promoted to packaging manager because of his work ethic and ability to get things done in half the time the previous manager had (he, too, was an Engineer—too bad). Bill was well-liked by all and was fun to be around, but he was mischievous in a fun way that you didn't know what he was going to do next. He was a Purdue graduate and obtained his MBA from U of L after joining the company. He started going to the Kentucky Derby with Bob and our group in 1973, and we enjoyed his company. Thereafter, he was like a member of the group that went to Keeneland on Bluegrass Stakes day, and we went every weekend during the spring and fall meet and usually came home a winner in those days of the '70s and '80s. We also went to other tracks out of town to ply our craft.

Since I was hired in 1956, the company had their annual Christmas parties. I attended my first one downtown at the Madrid Hotel, and it was a humdinger. They had a group of women employees that made up the dancing dolls, and they put on a can-can show, and the whiskey flowed like buttermilk. Most everyone was inebriated, and they handed out Christmas bonuses. One hourly worker punched our CEO in the abdomen as he handed him his check. I was stunned like everyone else, and the whole party ended up in a donnybrook, and they tore up the ball room and smashed the mirror behind the bar. It was a fiasco, and I ended up sitting on the curb at Third and Chestnut Streets. How I got home, I don't even know to this day. I must have taken a bus, but I took no part in any bad behavior. After that, the hourly employees had a separate party from the office personnel.

They then moved the next parties to the old Seelbach Hotel to the grand ballroom on the tenth floor. They always had an employee show, which was the highlight of the party, and many participated in it, but I was never part of the show. They had rehearsals before the party each year. In 1972, Bill, my buddy by then, was part of the performances in the show. It was usually very well done and gave the employee a chance to show off their other talents. During the rehearsal the night before, Bill drank too much and ended up with people he didn't even know. Anyway, he stayed up all night and was in bad shape for the party show the next day. His antics were a bit unorthodox and ended up in an alcohol-induced stupor. I told him I would take him home. His new car was in a nearby parking garage. We went down to the first floor on the elevator, but I had forgotten my overcoat and told him to stand there in the lobby until I retrieved my coat. When I came back, he was nowhere to be found. So I went out hunting for him in my car, and lo and behold, I saw a parking garage exit gate arm lying out in the street all smashed up. I knew right away what he had done. He apparently just crashed through the gate and kept going. How he got home is still a mystery, considering the alcohol-induced state he was in. The Christmas parties continued on and always produced unusual situations. I could go on and on about these parties, but I will leave that to your imagination.

Also during these early days, they had a summer picnic out on River Road, and there were some knock-down drag-out festivities. I always had my fill of booze and was active in playing the games, such as volleyball, softball, horseshoes, swimming, etc.; and I was most fortunate enough to stay out of serious trouble.

In 1973, we decided to visit Oaklawn Racetrack in Hot Springs, Arkansas. Bob, Bill, my father, and I all piled into Bob's truck camper and took off and traveled all night. We camped at KOA one night to get some sleep, and in the middle of the night, my father got up to relieve himself out of the back of the camper door. Not knowing where he was, he stepped out and fell into some large bushes directly behind the camper, and Bob rescued him. He was seventy-two at the time, and if it had not been for those heavenly bushes, he might have been seriously injured or dead. The next morning, Bob was up early and went to the community lavatory to wash up about 6:00 a.m., as was his lifelong habit. He was singing aloud "Georgia On My Mind." Since he had a loud carrying voice, you could hear him from a hundred yards away. He had an exceptional voice, and he had been singing ever since he was a youngster of fourteen years of age. He would break out in song at any time regardless where he was, and it was something to behold. He was one-of-a-kind and had a hard-scrabble existence growing up and always said, "I have to sing to keep from crying." He woke up the whole camping community absentmindedly, and they were all clapping as he strolled down the walkway in his underwear. Truly a sight to behold. My father always got a big kick out of Bob's singing, and when my father was on his death bed some years later in 1980, I was in the hospital room with my father and things were grim. He heard Bob coming down the hallway singing, and he broke out into a big grin. A fitting end and a wonderful experience. Bob lived across the street from us when I was ten years old. For about twenty years, you could hear him singing Al Jolson songs every day when he wasn't working in his father's carpenter shop. He was one of several children and lived a spartan existence. He would break out in song at any time and anywhere, even in the grocery store, and nearly everyone loved it. It was an unconscious habit, and you would have to see it and hear it to believe it!

We found the race track Oaklawn and went to bet for two days, and when we got there, a woman with a cigarette was standing next to Bill. She touched his new polyester pants with the lit cigarette and burned a hole in them—good way to start. Oaklawn then was a fairly new track, and since there was no race tracks in Texas at the time, a lot of Texans attended the races there. They had $100 betting windows, and we were amazed to see these farmers, ranchers, or whatever standing in the line at these windows to bet. The paddock was on the inside of the building, and it was hard to see the horses. To make a long story short, we lost money but not too much. We didn't bet the rent money. We made it home without much trouble, but one time like this was enough for all. Meanwhile, our wives kept the home fires burning, and I think they were glad to get respite from our presence for a few days.

Our label supplier, Bill, and I took another venture to the Fairgrounds in New Orleans in 1978, primarily to bet on Run Dusty Run who ran second in the Kentucky Derby to Seattle Slew in 1977. We stayed in a nice hotel in the outskirts of New Orleans and holed up Thursday and Friday to read the racing form, drink, and raise hell without getting kicked out. We had broke about even on Friday, but the big race on Saturday was a different story. We were almost certain that Run Dusty Run was going to win the New Orleans handicap. We bet all the money we had left, and he ran second even though he was the heavy favorite. Again, we forgot our old tried-and-true betting strategy and got creamed. We barely had enough money to eat dinner, and our supplier never let us forget this blunder. He was beat by a good horse named Cleaver Trick, which we overlooked. So much for that fiasco.

Some other noteworthy excursions that we took are as follows:

In the midseventies, our glass supplier rep Joe had football tickets to the Cincinnati Bengals; and Pat, Bill, and I were invited to go with him. Joe had a portable bar with all the trimmings that he had purchased, and we had a tailgate party before the game. Also, all of us had our own alcohol stash in our pockets. Much to our dismay, our seats were in the upper deck and looking down made one wonder if we were going to tumble down when we stood up. To say that we were inebriated during the game was an understatement. Pat brought along a pint of blackberry brandy, and we sipped on it throughout the game and all had purple tongues like a chow dog when the game was over. We had no idea who had won and didn't care. When we returned to the car, we again proceeded to partake of Joe's bar contents. By this time, I was doubtful that any of us would survive the night. Bill acquired the hiccups, so we had to stop at Big Bone Lick to accommodate him. We stopped right in front of the police department, which was closed—thank God!—and applied different methods of curing the hiccups. One of the solutions was to stick a dirty handkerchief down Bill's throat. Needless to say, that didn't work, so we had another drink, believe it or not, and took off for home. By this time, Joe had finally began to show his being in his cups, and we were all over the road. I was in the front passenger seat with him, trying to keep him awake and on the road. The other two were in the back, trying to keep from puking. Somehow, by the grace of God, we made it back without any incident. I understand that Joe had a bowling engagement that night with this team, which included his wife, and he bowled a forty-nine in the first game, and his wife was furious to say the least.

Later in the late '70s, Joe, Bill, and I went to the Cincinnati Reds game to see them play; and Joe still had his portable bar, but we pledged that we would not consume too much alcohol. We did fairly well; however, Bill and I were sitting in the box seat on the first base side about ten rows up the stadium when the Reds pitcher came to bat. He fouled a pitch off the end of his bat, and it came like a bullet right as us. We didn't even have a chance to duck or react. The ball fortunately hit the pipe bar of the box and saved one of us from a severe head injury. Again, we escaped unharmed. This time we were relatively sober.

Early in 1957, I was sent to Gas City, Indiana, to witness and learn how glass bottles were manufactured and to examine their inspection systems and establish some quality limit samples for the quality control lab to adhere to and see firsthand why glass bottle making was an <u>art</u> and not yet a science. We had numerous defective bottles arrive at our plant from the three glass suppliers that shipped glass to us. I drove there in my old Chrysler and stayed at an old hotel in Gas City. At the time, Gas City was the plant that made most of our bottles. I was met at the plant by the inspections supervisor, Dutch, who was a grizzly good ole boy who taught me what to look for when inspecting bottles. I learned a great deal from him, and his staff proved invaluable over the years. The first day was a grueling one, I think, on purpose for a young whippersnapper like me and being a city slicker, so to speak. Dutch was noted for his beer-drinking prowess, and they took me to their favorite watering hole. Over the course of the night, we must have drunk at least twelve beers a piece. While his staff (two others) quit. They thought that I would say uncle, but they didn't know my past drinking proclivities. They were surprised when I was still standing out in the parking lot in the rain, offering all a drink of our finest whiskey. When I turned up the next morning fresh as a daisy after about three hours of sleep, they were amazed at my constitution and endurance, and we became life-long friends. Again, my appearance was deceptive, and my demeanor, acquired as a boy, was unassuming, unpretentious, and unconcerned. It served me well throughout my life. Most everyone underestimated my strength and endurance. They always greeted me with respect after that episode. They changed their minds about city slickers after that trip.

In 1975, I again traveled to Alton, Illinois, by airplane with Joe to inspect a new decanter. It was one of our glass suppliers' largest plants. We experienced trouble with the panels of the bottle and spent a lot of time on the hot end, where temperatures were at least 110 degrees or more the closer we got to the molten glass. Anyway, we were in need of hydration, and we were glad when the work concluded. So we jumped into a rental car and drove to St. Louis, Missouri, to catch a flight home. I asked Joe to stop and get a six pack to replenish our systems with liquid. He said we would wait and visit the airport bar in St. Louis because we had a two- to three-hour wait before departure. The bar was on the upper floor overlooking the airport runway!

We made a beeline for this bar, and we were the only two people in there and decided we wanted vodka and tonic to quench our thirst. We were dehydrated, and he ordered a tall glass of vodka and tonic and gulped them down in almost five minutes. He kept ordering them and kept the waitress and bartender busy. I knew I was in trouble because Joe could really slurp alcohol down. We drank thirteen vodka and tonics (tall glasses) before we up got up to leave for the airport. When we got up to leave, the bartender and waitress clapped for us. We boarded the plane, and he immediately ordered a Jack Daniels. I refused rather than to puke. When we returned to Louisville, my wife and son picked us up, and Joe said to go to the bar for another drink. I was barely mobile, and my wife wondered what was wrong with me. I was green around the gills.

CHAPTER 13

Swale won the 1984 Kentucky Derby on a fast track, and the weather was overcast but good. He was owned by Claiborne Farm and ridden by Laffit Pincay Jr. and looked spectacular in the paddock. He was sired by Seattle Slew (1977) and Double Jay (four back) on the distaff and right down our pedigree alley. There were twenty horses in the race with a mutuel field (six horses) and two entries. We bet him to show, and he paid $8.80 to win and $3.40 to show. I always went down to the paddock from the host's box seats about thirty minutes before post. My wife, Doris, and another friend, Jim and his wife Alice, were in the box seats; and when they saw Swale walk in front of them, they started digging in their pockets to bet him. They bet every dollar they had, including some change, on him independent of me; and we all won and all were ecstatic and celebrated liberally. Swale was third down the back stretch in perfect position and took the lead at the mile pole and won easily by about three lengths. Picking him was relatively easy for a change. He went on to win the Belmont Stakes (1 ½ miles) that year, but died soon after due to a twisted intestine, and it was a real tragedy for Claiborne Farms. Again our hosts' put on a three-day affair in grand style, which consisted of dinners and brunches at the country club. Derby breakfast at the Jefferson Club, etc. Dick and Gloria were the most gracious hosts ever, and we thank them for that.

In April of 1985, I was invited by our glass supplier to attend a Masters golf tournament in Augusta, Georgia. Dick and I were met at the airport by their company plane with other company executives on Wednesday, and we flew to Augusta. We spent the days and nights at a beautiful home not far from the golf course. Our glass supplier (in the Dow 30) had access to most all the major events in the country, and they treated us like kings. I never thought that I would someday be privy to such attention and opportunities. They had access to the clubhouse and fraternized with the players at lunch on Thursday and Friday, a very rare thing to do. Not many companies had tickets and access to so many major events. We were given yellow shirts (Masters logo), and I bought a Masters logo sun visor cap that I still have along with many other souvenir hat and caps. Dick and I walked the course with the favorites, and I was exhausted at the end of the day. Before play began, each member of our party (ten) drew for a first pick and so on, and all put up $20 to be given to the winner who picked the champion.

On Sunday afternoon, we flew back, and they dropped us off. When we went home, we saw the rest of the Sundays' final eighteen holes live on TV. What a spectacular journey, and I was privileged to be part of it. We went back to the Masters tournament the next year, and more or less had the same experience. I wasn't a golfer, but I understood the ability it took to play the game and enjoyed the patience and versatility of those pro golfers. We had a great time, and I was more familiar with what was expected of me and conducted myself in a manner in keeping with my position as vice president director of purchasing.

Also during the years between '82 and '90, the same glass supplier owned a trout hatchery and fishing stream near Sandusky, Ohio, called Castalia Farms. They furnished trout hatchlings to farms all over the US. A part of this complex was meeting rooms, cottages, mess halls, etc. for corporate meetings and customers. An adjoining parcel of land called Milsite was the main customer fishing stream, with a lodge and living quarters all around. All the fishing equipment you would ever need was also furnished. They also had duck hunting at a nearby site. It was an unbelievable site, and they always invited a group of our employees to fly up there for the weekend. You could do what you wanted and had fishing contests for the most fish and largest trout caught, received the proceeds from everyone who participated, and had to put up $10 to go to the winner. I wasn't the best fisherman, and it took me several years to catch on to the right techniques. I finally did catch the largest tiger trout one year. My buddy Bill was very good at this and won the contest for most fish caught several times. It's hard to put into words the accommodations and hospitality that we enjoyed. They boxed up (iced) the catch, and each member of our group brought home at least a box of five large rainbow trout. They make a delicious meal. Our supplier thought of everything imaginable to satisfy anyone in the world. I'd never forget the times we spent at Milsite and the great camaraderie that ensued. A truly remarkable experience for a refugee kid like me. I didn't know such things existed, and me, of all people, to be part of it was unthinkable to me early on. Bill and I were well-liked, and even when we retired, we were invited back years later. They flew us up and back on their corporate plane with Bill's son to once again be treated like royalty. Later on, they closed and sold this complex during consolidations, takeover, going private, etc., and I don't know if it even exists anymore. A time that has <u>come</u> and <u>gone,</u> and I was lucky enough to be part of it.

In the meantime, my job as director became more intolerable with each passing year between 1983 and 1991, and I wished, even with all the above perks that went with the job, that I had never taken this job with all the expectations and new bosses (experts from out of town) that were hired and brought in supposedly to run the show. More on these pitiful people later.

There is no way that I can iterate all the episodes, good and bad, that I can convey in this writing, and I am just hitting the highlights that are most memorable. A few others are as follows:

Back around 1975, we had a glass salesman at the time call on us in quality control named Bill M. He was a very gregarious aggressive guy, but he had heard of our thoroughbred betting skills and dedicated aficionados, and believe it or not, he had won $35,000 on a pick six bet at Finger Lakes Race Track in upstate New York. He and his wife went to the track for fun, and he had no prior knowledge or desire to be a punter. They chose a series of numbers and bet $2 on a pick six that consisted of birthday, marriage dates, etc.'; and yes, you guessed it, they won, and he showed up a copy of the check that Finger Lakes track had paid him. We were astonished to say the least because that type of bet had just come into play that year. This was a form of lottery before lottery came into vogue. Bill and myself became friends, and he became hooked on betting horses. He was a crackerjack salesman and was very successful in that endeavor and earned big salaries at different corporations. He also later owned horses after going broke several times. He was a big better and lost all his money that he won earlier. He lived in Tampa, Florida, and quit gambling for a while. Then started back again and visited us five years ago at the Kentucky Derby. He passed away in 2018 at a too early age, but what a character. This is worth mentioning here because it shows the danger and problems that can occur when you become addicted to gambling, or anything else for that matter. We are all addicted to something!

I would be remiss if I didn't mention that my beautiful auburn-haired daughter decided to get married in June of 1974, and she had a wonderful wedding. I gave her away much to my dismay, but such is life. She had two children, Amber Dawn, my granddaughter, and Brandon Michael, my grandson, and we love them dearly. My daughter Deborah is a chip off the old block, except she is more moderate and sensible that most of my clan. She must have inherited traits from her mother, who stuck with me all these years (sixty-seven) in spite of outside-of-the-norm antics. Debbie has been a tremendous help over the years and still is assisting us in caring for our disabled son, who fell three hundred feet off a bluff cliff when he was nineteen years old. Without her, we would not be able to cope with this horrible calamity, and we are so proud of her and her two children. That is hard to put into words. She is a survivor with an innate sense and aptitude that defied a logical explanation. She will be our power of attorney in the days to come—like soon, if she, of course, agrees. I feel confident that her decisions in the future will be invaluable to the whole family. I started with very little, as she did, and accomplished more through perseverance and the insightful heritage that has been passed down through the years to keep our unique persona alive and well. Her married name is Sims, but she is a take-no-prisoners Sutton down to the core.

In April of 1958, my first son and secondborn, Francis Eugene Sutton, was named after his great-grandfather, who was the smithy alluded to earlier. He was a whopper of a child, and everything came easy for him as a youngster. He grew big and strong and was always ahead of the crowd. He was a star basketball player in elementary school, to say the least, and also an all-star on the Little League baseball team but wasn't aware of it or acted like it. He tried out for the basketball team in high school, but severely broke his tibia and fibula when some goon undercut him as he was shooting a jump shot, a spiral fracture (break) that took almost a year to heal. He was never the same athlete after that episode. He worked as a handyman where we lived when he was seventeen and eighteen and attended college for three and a half years before other factors raised their ugly heads. I got him a part-time job at the company where I worked, and he later became a full-time employee. When he was eighteen, he started to drink some, but it soon got out of hand because of the perceived macho syndrome it portrayed. Since he was of our clan, he morphed into a heavy drinker. He found out since he could drink more than his cronies that he was a macho man on campus, so to speak. This eventually led to his dismissal from his job. He has had some hard times recovering from years of heavy drinking. He fought his way back, and he is okay now! He also slipped on some black ice while unloading groceries and broke his hip. This happened at night, and no one saw him lying there on the street. He dragged himself into his house in a herculean effort and called us, and we then called EMS, and he was laid up for two years and still cannot bend over or walk normally. Another near tragedy that had to be dealt with.

I finally acquired a decent car in 1968, a 1966 Dodge that was my uncle's until he passed, and I purchased it from his estate because it was in such good condition and not been driven much.

I was on my way home from work on December 23, 1968, on vacation for the holidays. About 5:00 p.m., an old man in an old truck turned into me as I was going through a green light. There was a grocery store on that corner, and I was heading straight for it, but the curbing and sewer cap on the corner was sunk, so the curb protruded up about twelve to fifteen inches, and I hit it first and careened away from the grocery store, which was crowded with black personnel who lived in that area. It just so happened that I was able to steer the car with the wheels on the street and two wheels on the sidewalk. A black woman was walking on the sidewalk coming toward me, and I was able to turn the wheel away from her and back onto the street, saving her from serious injury or death. It just so happened that the blacks in Louisville were rioting against discrimination at the time. I tried to flag down two police cars, but they pretended not to see the accident because they didn't want to get involved in a possible riot scene. Immediately, my adrenaline kicked in to save myself. There was numerous witness to the accident (old man's fault), and they surrounded me in a matter of seconds. My quick thinking and my ability to avoid running over the woman saved me from being mobbed. I confidently walked into the store that I would have crashed into if not for the high curb that changed the direction of the car and called my father, and he came down and picked me up. My car was almost totaled but was repaired, but it was never the same. My quick thinking saved her life and my skin. Never again do I trust the police to do anything.

In 1982, Chris and Barbara H. took us on trip to New York City. Chris worked for another glass supplier at the time, and we always enjoyed their company. He had previously made reservations and arraignments, and we landed in NYC and proceeded to take a tour of the city and stayed in the Plaza Hotel overlooking Central Park. The next day, we went down to the first floor to grab a bite to eat for lunch. The prices on the menu were out of this world, and I refused to pay that much for a single hamburger and a coke; it was outrageous. We then went to Tavern on the Green in Central Park on a beautiful day and thoroughly enjoyed the ambiance of the place. The next day, we decided to go to the Metropolitan Museum of Art, which we had never seen. It was a great experience, and I bought a print duplicate of "Salome," a two by four 1870 painting by H. Regnault, a noted artist of Rome. They all laughed at me because it was so large, and they wondered how I was going to bring it home.

When we left the museum, Murphy's law kicked in, and it started pouring down rain. I rolled the painting up and stuck in under my coat and down my pants. We finally hailed a cab that was driven by a man from Ghana. When he found out we were just going back to the Plaza, which was close by, he shouted at us to get out! There was a parade going on, and he was furious because he wasn't going to make enough money on the quick ride to the hotel. Fortunately, it had stopped raining (pouring down and soaking), and we made our way back to the hotel with my painting intact even though I had to walk and sit at a particular angle in order to protect my painting. I had it framed when we returned home, and as I sit here in our den, I'm looking at it with fond memories. It is a great piece of art that everyone asks about to this day.

CHAPTER 14

Doris & John Sutton – Kentucky Derby – 1986

Spend a Buck won the 1985 Kentucky Derby on a clear day and a fast track and paid $10.70 to win, with Angel Cordero in the irons. The big favorite, Chief's Crown, ran third and paid $2.80 to show, and that's who we bet to show. Spend a Buck led from the start, and no one was going to catch him that day. We bet Chief's Crown because he was a two-year-old champion and had good breeding. We won on the day and even won on the show parley that I managed for the group of eighteen, so all were well pleased. By this time, our host had to have me along because everyone else was a novice concerning horse racing, so I was much in demand, and that's not an easy task by no means. I can only talk to one or two people at a time, and if I suggested to them a horse to bet on and it lost, you would think that I committed larceny. Tough job, but somebody has got ———."

This was the first time that Churchill Downs allowed exotic betting on the derby, and that was just on an <u>exacta</u>. The old cardboard tickets and many windows one had to navigate came to an end with the advent of the computerized pari-mutuel tickets, and oh! What a relief that was for people like me. It made betting a pleasure, rather than a chore with long lines.

On May 3, 1986, Ferdinand won the Kentucky Derby on a chilly but clear day, and the track was designated as fast. There were sixteen horses in the race, and Ferdinand had post position #1. With that many horses in the race, the #1 post position was not favorable because you could get pinched in due to all the others coming over to the rail to obtain a good position going into the first turn, which is advantageous inasmuch as you wouldn't have to go wide going into the first turn and lose ground. However, Ferdinand, ridden by Willie Shoemaker and trained by Charlie Whittingham, fell back and did not contend for the lead. He improved his position steadily on the back stretch and won by two-plus lengths going away and paid $37.40 to win. He ran second in the Preakness and third in the Belmont. We totally miscalculated his ability and lost big time for a change.

This setback was a blow to my ego, and I started to think about a more systematic approach to find a well-bred steed that one could bet on as a long shot as we did in 1967 with Proud Clarion. Ferdinand was well-bred and sired by Nijinsky II, who was sired by the great Northern Dancer and out of a Double Jay mare, which showed impeccable breeding. I was dismayed that I overlooked this information and vowed to not let this happen again. All the razzle-dazzle and socializing I had to do was beginning to take a toll on my judgment.

In the meantime, during the '80s, starting in 1981, our group of seven people rented a houseboat at Cumberland Lake near the Tennessee border the week after Labor Day for three days of fun and games. The rental fee after Labor Day was much less than before Labor Day, and we took advantage of that, and also the weather wasn't so hot. Our first trip was to Grider Hill Marina, so we all left home in two cars loaded with food and booze, looking forward to some good times. Bill and I and our wives were in one, and Neil, Tina, and Jim were in the other car. We got separated on the way down (150 miles), and we arrived around noon at Grider Hill. The other car got lost and ended up in Tennessee before they realized their mistake. The road and entrance to the marina was situated on a steep hill, and we had to unload and carry all our supplies down to the dock and onto the boat. Unfortunately, all the booze was in the other car. It was hot that day, and we were having alcohol withdrawals as we sat waiting for the others to arrive with one 1/10th pint (airplane drink) available between us and were desperate for some booze. About two hours later, the other car arrived, and we quickly unloaded the car and set off to find a cove to pitch anchor. Before we got out of the marina, we had consumed a 1.75 liter of vodka to quench our thirsts. We had to make up for lost time. We finally found a cove to anchor and donned our swimsuits, rafts, etc. to revel around the area. We even had a separate raft that was tethered that held bottles and glasses so we could drink at will, and so we did.

Later we grilled large filet steaks and all the trimmings to satisfy our hunger. As one of our group was turning the 16 oz. steaks over, he flipped one of them into the lake, and the fish never left our boat side after that boo-boo. No one cared because we were just there on holiday to have fun. Later that night, you could see the stars very clearly, and our amateur stargazer (Neil) was showing us the Big and Little Dipper, etc. As he pointed out the Cassiopeia constellation, he was standing on the rail and lost his footing and came crashing down among all the lawn chairs and chaise lounges, and all snapped shut like mouse traps. We had to disentangle him from the melee. He wasn't hurt, but he looked to be in a state of shock, and we never let him forget his humpty-dumpty fall. We kept drinking and couldn't get enough. I consumed about a quart of bourbon on top of all the vodka we had drunk during the day, and the next morning after about two hours of sleep, I thought I was going to die from alcohol poisoning, as my buddy Bill tried to force a beer down my throat to help me. It took me most of the day to recover and never again was I going to endanger my life like that.

We continued to go to Grider Hill for two more years but the loading and unloading of supplies on that steep incline changed our minds, and for the remainder of the decade, we went to Burnside Marina, which was much closer and easier to negotiate the terrain.

Each time we went, we encountered a number of unbelievable circumstances, and each one was an adventure unto itself. Wild Bill was usually our pilot, and by the grace of God, we made it safely back and forth.

Doris & John – Cumberland Lake – Circa 1983

On one occasion, in our haste to leave the marina for open water, he gunned the new motor on a sixty-foot houseboat, and the engine blew up. We had to call for help, and the personnel from the marina had to remove and replace the blown motor with a new one. It took about two to three hours, and we were sweltering in the heat and proceeded to consume a staggering amount of ethyl alcohol. We always managed to find a good cove to pitch anchor and tie up. In the mornings, we always went to the nearest marina, like Conley Bottom, and had a huge breakfast of eggs, ham, bacon, biscuits, and white gravy that helped to counteract our alcohol overindulgence. There were many more episodes through the decade that were as unusual as the aforementioned ones at Cumberland Lake that were noteworthy I could reiterate and may do so later.

When I took over the Purchasing Department in mid-1983 as director, I set about trying to obtain a price reduction on all our supplies, unknown to my bosses. He had been shuffled around in different areas to supposedly learn or be acquainted with other departments. It so happened that he landed in the production services area. Marketing, sales administration, human resources, etc. did not want him meddling in their business, so they sent him over to us as usual. The company reorganized at the time, and we became part of the corporate subsidiaries. Since we were short one person, we hired Lou, an experienced packaging man from a local company. I had to fight like hell to keep human resources from hiring an ex-serviceman minority navy supply person who wasn't qualified for the job I had in mind. I had been dealing with our bottling suppliers for twenty-five years, and I knew that I would negotiate with them because of my good relationships with them. My unbiased appraisal of their products over the years was an asset to them and to us. Lou and I combined to put our glass bottles, our largest expense up for bids. We had three glass suppliers at that time, and I knew each of their branch managers intimately, and they knew that I was hardnosed enough to pit one against the other as to delegate or retract more business from them in an honest bidding contest. Never before in the history of the company has anyone—at least since after World War II—been able to put our glass purchases up for bids, which included my two predecessors, who had been there since then and was smart and honest directors who built the Purchasing Department to what it was and introduced checks and balances to ward off any improprieties. More on that later!

In any event, our bidding was successful, and we had a price reduction from all our glass suppliers that saved the company 4 million dollars per year, ad infinitum. Three years later, I asked our main glass supplier at the Kentucky Derby to consider cost savings on glass and that we needed some relief. They willingly agreed, and another savings of approximately 4 million dollars was forthcoming. Never <u>before</u> and never <u>after</u> my tenure as director had this been accomplished and was a spectacular achievement for everyone. I wasn't adequately compensated for this endeavor, and I resented it, as others in other entities of corporate standing dithered and whiled away their time sucking up to their supervisors and playing golf, etc., to impress their cohorts. My predecessor, who worked diligently for forty years and was underpaid for his efforts, and that also rankled me. If he had not adamantly campaigned for me to replace him, they would and were going to hire an *expert* from outside the company, which was a policy that most corporations were undertaking. Why? God only knows! My experience and education qualified me, especially since I was the <u>only</u> employee among the many who possessed a master's degree in mathematics, a one-of-a kind and unique achievement in the corporation. Don knew that I was the only one capable of running the Purchasing Department due to my past association with our materials, suppliers, and analytical determinations. I had been doing this for twenty-five years and was adept at troubleshooting and solving bottling line difficulties that occurred daily. Bill, who was now my good friend, was the only other person in the corporation capable of handling that job, but he saw the handwriting on the wall and did not want this onerous <u>job,</u> so it fell in my lap, so to speak. I was relatively satisfied as quality control manager and was not seeking any promotions, etc., because, as I earlier stated, I wasn't one to kiss ass, and I know that was what was required in the next step up the ladder. I could not bring myself to acquire the brown ring around my nose, which would have been a disgrace to my ancestors and DNA. The corporate leaders call this today kissing butt as being <u>mature,</u> but I say it is a bunch of manure. If that's the <u>only way</u> to be a leader, then forget me. I know better because I had always been a leader by natural traits and didn't need this type of crap, but nonetheless, this seems to be the American corporations MO. I respect and follow orders of my superiors as I did for the fifty-five years and was sought after in the US Army, which none of our top executives served, probably due to their daddies getting them deferred for some made-up medical exemption such as bone spurs on their heel. They know nothing about respect, discipline, and camaraderie. So be it—so let's hear it for the <u>boys</u>.

Doris & John – Kentucky Derby 1987

At the same time of my 1983 promotion, our CEO had plans to do away with many purchasing and accounts payable personnel as possible by introducing a computerized AP/PO system, and it didn't take me long to figure out their hidden agenda. To implement this system, it required some technical know-how to accomplish. In other words, work myself out of a job. One month after I took over, corporate sent one of their VPs in the Accounting Department with a pathetic justification for implementation of this system. Wanting me to sign off on a phony made-up statistical analysis of how much money would be saved by going computerized. They did not mention or imply in any way to me that the <u>real</u> <u>purpose</u> of this accounts payable/purchase order system was to eliminate about ten people from their payroll and benefits accrued by them, including me. Their pathetic scheming did not go unnoticed by me as a hidden agenda of people that I learned as a boy from my father's all-night sessions, and that was an integral part of my modus operandi. I refused to accept their justification, which you had to offset the cost of purchasing the system, and that, in the end, cost over 1 million dollars. This refusal of their concocted justification apparently did not set well with the CEO and his cohorts. They expected me to fall in line with the rest of their lackeys, so new tactics were hatched to induce me to acquiesce.

Alysheba won the 1987 Kentucky Derby on a warm but cloudy day on a fast track. There were seventeen horses in the race, and he rallied to beat Bet Twice after stumbling slightly in the stretch. He had won the Bluegrass Stakes in his previous race but was disqualified and ran third. He was sired by Alydar (out of a War Admiral mare, four back). He had an epiglottis operation about three weeks before the derby, which opened up his breathing, and he blossomed out. We bet him to win and loaded up on him to show. Needless to say, we were ecstatic over our good fortune, especially having lost the previous year. He paid $18.80 to win and $6.20 to show. Need I say that a celebration ensued? He went on to win the Preakness and Super Derby as a three-year-old colt. Bob, who was my early buddy, no longer could go with us but nevertheless we consulted with him, and he also bet through a bookie at the American Legion. He was busy sending his three girls through Catholic High School and U of L in the '80s, and money was a precious commodity that he needed to sustain them.

Top - Bluegrass Stakes Program– 1988 – with all Jockey
signatures (Prep Race for Ky Debry) Bottom – Ky Derby Program
with all Jockey signatures – for Winning Colors (Filly)

On May 7, 1988, Winning Colors won the Kentucky Derby on a beautiful clear day and on a fast track. She was only the third filly to win the derby. She was huge and bigger than all the other colts. Her roan coat shown brilliantly in the paddock, and she had that look. We knew she was ready to run. She had won the Santa Anita Derby easily, but we knew the odds of a filly winning a race of 1 ¼ miles even though she was allowed a five-pound weight advantage, and that was what won the race for her. She took the lead right out of the gate from the #11 post position and never looked back. She had speed to burn and won by a neck over the fast-closing Forty Niner with Pat Day (our favorite jockey) aboard. She was ridden by Gary Stevens and trained by D. Wayne Lucas. We bet Private Terms to show, and he ran out of the money (ninth), so we lost and were disappointed that we did not bet the winner, because she looked so good in the paddock. She ran third in the Preakness and was unplaced in the Belmont. The derby took a lot out of her, and she was never the same again. The derby takes a lot of a horse, and that's why it's so difficult to win the Triple Crown.

In 1989, my relationship with the CEO soured, and I was on the hit list. I knew it since I was approaching the dangerous age of sixty in the corporate world, but they were underestimating my moxie of what made the merry go, as my father often said. Most of my cohorts of early years had already been dismissed, and we had these out-of-town experts running the show, and they had no clue of what was holding production together, and I wasn't about to tell them because it was an engineer, Jerry, and myself that was the glue that kept the lines humming. I had spent twenty-five years solving bottling line problems and interacting with our material suppliers, and these new dodos didn't know that, and they never sought my advice. They were trying what they thought were fresh ideas, but didn't know that those ideas had already been tried and failed. I could see the train wreck coming, and so be it. They had already failed in several projects. They hired several PhDs to implement this new venture and acquired some land near the Cumberland River. They had expanded the laboratory in the Reagan era because they could write off in taxes any research and development costs. They were all about acquiring new ventures and spent millions trying to do so. One of my good friends, Jim, a chemical engineer, had previously advised them to acquire an alcohol-related business based in St. Louis, Missouri, and it fit into the company's expertise. They made other attempts to branch out but didn't do the research to be successful. They made many other boo-boos like the acquisition of a cooler company during the cooler craze of the '80s. Again, those that were responsible did not shoulder any blame and in fact were rewarded for their failures through bonuses, etc. Let a lesser paid employee make those kinds of mistakes and they would have been dismissed or demoted. If you can understand that type of logic, then you got me beat.

Kentucky Derby 1989 – Jefferson Club brunch – Doris and John Sutton

Sunday Silence won the 1989 Kentucky Derby on a muddy track made worse by intervals of sleet, and it was cold and overcast. He was ridden by P. Valenzuela and trained by Charlie Whittingham and paid $8.20 to win. He won the Santa Anita Derby and the Preakness, and was second in the Belmont Stakes and won the Breeders' Cup classic that year. He ran fourth most of the way and took command during the stretch run to win by two lengths. We bet Easy Goer to show, who was the odds-on favorite, and ran second in an entry and looked to be unbeatable. He paid $3.40 to show because his entry mate ran third, making the show payoff more that the place payoff. We were happy with the result. Sunday Silence was sired by Halo, who in turn was sired by Hail to Reason, who was one of the top breeding stallions of the past years; but we passed him up because of the entry and because Easy Goer was a two-year-old champion. We were with our glass suppliers, as hosts, and I went down to the paddock to see the horses, as usual, thirty minutes before post time. I won a considerable amount of money, and one of our new VPs got ticked off because I won and he lost. So I spent $50 on drinks at the bar to soothe the savage beast who was short on common sense. He later got shipped out to a subsidiary and passed away later. Another expert from out-of-town down the drain. Others would soon follow after I retired. That's the kind of crap I was dealing with. I would have told him what to bet on if he would have asked me. He thought he knew as much about horse racing as I did. He knew absolutely zilch about anything except himself. To top it all off, his inebriated wife spilled a glass of red wine on my wife's new $300 dress.

Another noteworthy incident occurred while traveling on a bus to the Kentucky Derby with eighteen people aboard. There were six of us from our company and twelve others from the host company supplier, and others. We had been to the Oaks the day before and had assembled at the country club for our trip to the Derby (thirty minutes). I had won on Oaks day and was attempting to read the daily racing form for all nine races on Derby Day. Besides being guests, my wife and I were expected to socialize and be congenial and answer questions from most of them about the derby, etc. My boss had a racing form for the first time and didn't know squat about reading it. People were counting on me to help with their selections, bets, etc. One of our executives sat down beside me and asked me to show him how to read the racing form on the way to the track.

I had been reading the daily racing form for fifty years, but there is no way on earth that I could teach him how to read it in thirty minutes. He had two days before to learn, but he chose to ask me to show him how to in thirty minutes. I couldn't teach Albert Einstein in that time span. He still didn't get it when I told him other people wanted to converse with me, and I told him to look in the index and they explain all the abbreviated words and symbols. This was the kind of things I was dealing with not only then but also at work. *Experts!* At what? Good grief!

On May 5, 1990, Unbridled won the Kentucky Derby on a drizzly overcast day and on a track classified as good. He was sired (two back) by Mr. Prospector and had won the Florida Derby. He won easily by about three lengths and was trained by Carl Nafgzer and was owned by Francis Genter, a ninety-year-old widow with a big stable. The famous photo of Carl and Francis hugging each other as Unbridled crossed the finish line was one for the books. He paid $23.60 to win. We bet Mister Frisky, who had won the Santa Anita Derby in his last outing. He ran eighth, and we bombed out and went to celebrate anyway. This derby was my last official one with our supplier, and I actually was glad of that even though the perks were outstanding. I was tired of being the go-to guy. Socializing and betting horses is hard to do, but I did it for ten years, and I was happy that it was over for the time being.

Over these ten years, our hosts, Dick and Jerry, couldn't have been more gracious; and I thank them for all the hard work and planning it takes to host sixteen people. I was not capable of this kind of effort and will forever be grateful that we were able to participate in such endeavors. We have pictures and photos of these grand events that led up to Derby Day, and we have fond memories of all those involved in these once-in-a lifetime events.

Strike the Gold won the 1991 Kentucky Derby on a cloudy day and on a fast track by about two lengths. He broke from the gate slowly but improved his position gradually until he was second at the stretch (1 mile) and finished strongly with Chris Antley in the irons and paid $11.60 to win. I bet on Hansel, who finished way back, and the distance proved to be his undoing. I was beginning to have second thoughts about my selection process.

I went to the derby with my oldest son, Eugene, and we went on the bus and had a great time in the paddock. Incidentally, he bet on the winner and was as happy as I've seen him in a long time, and we drank our share of booze throughout the day and night.

Strike the Gold was sired by Calumet's great sire, Alydar, who had the famous duels with Affirmed in the Kentucky Derby, Preakness, and Belmont Stakes in 1978. Alydar's breeding was from the Native Dancer line. Strike the Gold had won the Bluegrass Stakes earlier, and I would have kicked myself if I could to have overlooked all the signs that stared me in the face. We had a great time, however, and this was the only time was I able to be with my son at the derby. It was a special time indeed, and I'll never forget it.

On May 2, 1992, Lil E. Tee won the Kentucky Derby on a cloudy, drizzly day but on a track listed as fast. He was ridden by our favorite jockey, Pat Day, his one and only Kentucky Derby winner even though he was one of the greatest jockeys of all time. There were eighteen horses in the race, and Lil E. Tee had post position #10, a good post, and relaxed nicely coming out of the gate. He steadily improved his position and was gaining on the leaders with every stride and won by about a length. His breeding was somewhat suspect, but he was primed by Lynn Whiting, his trainer, to be at his best on Derby Day. That, of course, was the objective of every trainer. He paid a whopping $35.60 to win, and the chalk payers got fooled that day, including us. He had won a prep race, the Jim Beam at Latonia, an old race track in Kentucky near Cincinnati, Ohio, and ran second in the Arkansas Derby earlier; but he was overlooked by most of the expert handicappers, so what else was new?

We bet Arazi, who had won the Breeders' Cup Juvenile in 1991. We were there that day and saw him make a tremendous run around all the others to win going away. We vowed then and there that we were going to bet him in the derby next year if he ran. The Juvenile was 1 1/16 miles, and the derby is 3/16th of a mile longer. We found out the hard way that extra distance was not to his liking!

In 1989, we purchased a lot at Rough River Lake about ninety miles from Louisville. I saw an ad in the paper of the lots for sale, and we went down one weekend to view. We finally found one that had not even been cleared, and we couldn't see the water so the developer and us walked down through the thick underbrush to see it unfortunately, and when we got home, we both had the worst case of chiggers that you can imagine. The bites were <u>everywhere,</u> and both of us suffered greatly. In any event, we purchased the lot on the condition that they would run water to the lot. The object of our purchase was to have a place where our sons could go and get away from their cronies. Needless to say, neither one of them wanted to visit or stay because there was too much work involved to keep the place up.

We had a house built on the lot the next year, and so they started to build four other houses on the adjoining lots. To make a long story short, the developer was operating on a shoestring and the houses he built were lacking, to say the least; and we were constantly repairing or correcting his work for the next twenty-five years. I can't tell you how much shoddy work he did and failed to complete. He still is a developer in the Louisville area, and if you plan to deal with him, let the buyer beware. However, our Cumberland Lake group of four couples started to come down to the lake on our annual outing in lieu of going to Cumberland, which was very expensive, and had great times at Rough River that we all remember to this day. I finally sold the house, boat, etc. in 2017, and oh! What a relief.

Sea Hero won the 1993 Kentucky Derby on a cloudy day and on a fast track ridden by Jerry Bailey. There were nineteen horses in the race, and Sea Hero, trained by Mack Miller, came out of the #6 post position. He was unhurried early and commenced a rally between horses leaving the back stretch, moved inside the leaders for the drive, and drew clear to win by two-plus lengths. He had won the Champagne Stakes as a two-year-old and went on to win the Travers Stakes at Saratoga after the Derby, but he was unplaced in the Preakness and Belmont. He was highly bred having Danzing (two back) and Northern Dancer (three back) on the top side and the great Graustark and Ribot on the distaff. He paid $27.80 to win and $8.00 to show, and we bet him big time to change our recent luck. This was the beginning of a good winning streak.

After our recent losses, Bill and I developed a mathematical profile that was based on every past performance statistic available to us in the daily racing form that required a two-day accumulation of facts and averaged figures and ranked them accordingly. Sea Hero was our #1 selection. It incorporated other proven derby criteria as well, and we thought we had finally found the pot of gold and were giddy with success. We regained our confidence and were riding high. We set about fine-tuning our newly found system and could hardly wait for the 1994 Kentucky Derby to again cash in.

Go for Gin won the 1994 Kentucky Derby on a rainy day, and the track was sloppy with Chris McCarron in the saddle and trained by Nick Zito. There were fourteen horses in the race, and Go for Gin came out of post #8. He took the lead shortly after the first turn and never looked back winning by two lengths and paid $20.20 to win and $5.80 to show. This was the first year they allowed Trifecta betting on the Kentucky Derby. Our new analytical system ranked him #1, and we again scored a big-time win. He had won the Remsen Stakes (1 1/8 mile) as a two-year-old and was second in the Wood Memorial in an even race prior to the derby, which was a good indicator. Holy Bull was the big favorite that day and ran out of the money (twelfth). As the horses were parading out of the paddock, my semi-inebriated friend, Bill, shouted out so everyone could hear that Holy Bull was going down, and he did. Go for Gin was highly bred colt sired by Ribot (three back) out of Stage Door Johnny mare and fit right in with our analysis.

I was hired by a big pharmaceutical company to give a lecture on how to win the Kentucky Derby. I accompanied their group to Churchill Downs on Oaks Day on Friday to assist those who wanted my advice on betting. There were about fifty to seventy-five personnel located under a big tent that Churchill Downs farmed out inside of gate 10 with other tents and corporate tenants. I went with them on a bus from the Galt House, and it rained cats and dogs all day. Earlier before, we left the Galt House. I gave a lecture to those present (twenty) about how to go about picking the winner, etc., and before we left for the track, I wrote in big letters on the blackboard "GO FOR GIN," who was my pick for tomorrow's derby. I stayed with them under the tent all day Friday and attempted to help those that were unfamiliar with betting. The weather was so bad that most of them didn't care, but I went around to each table and offered my advice, as I was paid to do, but many weren't interested. I also won that day and gave them the derby winner.

When I retired in 1991, our production and production service leaders went about screwing up the apple cart big time, so I heard. Since I had negotiated two large cost savings from our largest supplier amounting to 8 million dollars per year, ad infinitum, they thought if I could do it, why couldn't they? After all, they were experts at nothing. They found another supplier and gave them some business thinking it would bring another cost savings. They replaced me with the packaging manager who knew absolutely zilch about purchasing anything, but of course, our leaders knew even less. They made a big mistake because the new supplier was not able to produce a quality product, and bottling efficiency went down the drain. They didn't know it, but Lou and I were holding everything together by a thin string, and when I left, every decision that was made was *wrong*. My replacement had a heart attack, and Lou's replacement had a nervous breakdown and had to quit. All I can say is that I knew that production would suffer, and so they did, and they had to send my friend, Jim, over to bail them out; but it took a while, and I don't think they ever really recovered. I was so glad to get out of the hornet's nest of know-nothings that I could barely contain myself. They deserved every bit of their misery. A fitting end to my thirty-five-year career, twenty-five of which I thoroughly did enjoy. The last ten years was a test of perseverance combating the schemers and know-nothings. The $8 million dollars per year cost savings that was never before or after enacted amounts to more than 250 million dollars of savings to date, and I doubt that will ever be consummated again. I was grossly underpaid for my contributions over the years. I would site many other significant contributions while I was materials quality control manager, which was contributory to the welfare of the company, but I will leave that for another place and time.

CHAPTER 15

Thunder Gulch won the 1995 Kentucky Derby on a partly cloudy day on a fast track. He was trained by D. W. Lucas and ridden by Gary Stevens, the same combination that won the 1988 Derby on Winning Colors (filly). He was regally bred with Raise a Native (three back) sire line out of a Storm Bird mare. He had won the Remsen Stakes at two and the Fountain of Youth and Florida Derby at three prior to the derby, but was overlooked in the derby and paid $51 to win. My grandson, Brandon Sims, was nine years old, and when he wanted a long shot to root for and bet on, I gave him Thunder Gulch, believe it or not, but I didn't bet on him myself. We did, however, bet Timber Country to show (Pat Day), who paid $3.80 to show, and we came out winner on the day.

There were nineteen horses in the race, and Thunder Gulch came out of the sixteenth hole (post), a first-time winner from that post position. He was out of the gate in good order, was reserved while within striking distance, and made a run four-wide approaching the stretch and won going away to win by a couple of lengths. Our system worked for us, inasmuch as pointing out our bet to show (Timber Country), which was a strategy we always had employed. Bill and I drank our modest amount of brain juice that day to keep with tradition and, of course, congratulated ourselves.

On May 4, 1996, Grindstone won the Kentucky Derby on an overcast day on a fast track and was owned by Overbook Farms and ridden by Jerry Bailey. He was sired by the 1990 winner Unbridled out of a mare by Drone and won the Louisiana Derby and was second in the Arkansas Derby. There were nineteen horses in the race, and

Grindstone came out of the #15 post position. He broke slowly and commenced to rally approaching the end of the backstretch and came between horses along the inside around the far turn, angled out very wide when entering the stretch, and finished strong to catch Cavonnier in the final stride to win by the hair on his nostrils and paid $13.80 to win. I don't think I have seen a closer finish in the Kentucky Derby, and it took a while for the stewards to determine a winner. This was a huge disappointment for Bob Baffert, who thought he had won. His horse had been struck across the face by a whip by Craig Perret, and that would have prevented him from winning even though the blow was unintentional. We bet Unbridled Song who took the lead briefly but faded to fifth during stretch run. Our winning streak had come to an end, but we knew our system was sound and that there is no such thing as a fool-proof horse betting system you could win on every time. We celebrated our defeat in our customary way and recovered slightly in the race following the Derby.

Silver Charm won the 1997 Kentucky Derby on a cool day with intermittent showers, and the track was listed as fast. Silver Charm was owned by Mr. and Mrs. Robert Lewis and trained by Bob Baffert and ridden by Gary Stevens. He was a roan colt and sired by Silver Buck out of a Poker mare. He ran second in the Santa Anita Derby a month earlier, and Bob had him primed for the Kentucky Derby. He paid $10 to win; he ran a rather even race and beat Captain Bodgit by a head in a stretch duel. This was Baffert's redemption from the previous year and the real emergence of Bob Baffert as a top-notch trainer. Before turning to thoroughbred racing, he was a quarter horse trainer and introduced new training techniques for his stable. Soon after, he was obtaining highly bred animals from the biggest farms and owners. New methods of training young horses started to catch on, and rather than run them often as two-year-olds, they took their time and trained them up for a race and late in their two-year-old season, if at all. He went on to win the Preakness and was second in the Belmont Stakes. We bet Captain Bodgit to show, so we were back again on the winning end. Silver Charm went on to win six more races in 1998 as a four-year-old and as the odds-on favorite in five of them. The system and heart medicine (100 proof) worked for us again.

On May 2, 1998, Real Quiet won the Kentucky Derby on an overcast day and on a fast track. He was a bay colt sired by Quiet American out of a Believe It mare and owned by Mike Pegram and again trained by Bob Baffert, who seems to have found the right formula for winning this iconic race. He had started nine times as a two-year-old, which was highly unusual especially for Baffert and had run second in the Santa Anita Derby just four weeks earlier. He then went on to win the Preakness with relative ease and was second in the Belmont Stakes losing by just a nose, or he would have been a Triple Crown winner. Many others have failed by a slim margin to win the Triple Crown. He was ridden by Kent Desormeaux in all his three-year-old races. He apparently blossomed out at the right time. His breeding was not exceptional but rather mediocre and was overlooked by many, including us, and he paid $18.80 to win with Victory Gallup running second and Indian Charlie ran third. He had a Beyer rating of 107 in the Santa Anita Derby and repeated that in the Kentucky Derby. We total overlooked these Beyer ratings and bet Indian Charlie to show. We broke about even but were disgusted with ourselves for not paying attention to his last two races before the derby. He was voted champion three-year-old colt. We had our usual ration.

Charismatic won the 1999 Kentucky Derby on a beautiful day and on a fast track. He was owned by Mr. and Mrs. Robert Lewis and trained by D. Wayne Lucas. He won only one race as a two-year-old and did not show much promise and was in a $62,500 claiming race as a three-year-old. He came to hand late and won the Lexington Stakes at Keeneland on April 18, the last prep race before the big one on May 1. He was ridden by C. Antley and won by a neck over Menifee. It showed once again that if a horse is feeling his oats, he is ready to run. He paid $62.60 to win, and we did not bet him and lost. He also won the Preakness and was third in the Belmont Stakes. He was declared the champion three-year-old colt and horse of the year. It sort of put a damper on our past performance calculations even though he had a 108 Beyer rating in the Lexington. He blossomed out at the right time probably due to the trainer extending him, as a two-year-old and early in his three-year-old campaign. Everyone that didn't have a hat on got a good dose of sunburn that day. We recovered in about an hour and iterated the loser's incantation. Wait till next year! And so we did, and we went on to celebrate our bad luck.

On May 6, 2000 (Y2K), Fusaichi Pegasus won the Kentucky Derby on a mostly sunny day over a fast track in 2:01.1, which was actually the second fastest time since Secretariat, who held the record time for the Kentucky Derby for twenty-seven years to date. He was owned by F. Sekiguchi and trained by Neil Drysdale and was regally bred by Mr. Prospector out of a Danzig mare (a complete outcross) and was a handful to handle and train—sort of a rogue, if you will. He would rear up and try to run off, and he had to be taken in hand by the rider and also by a lead pony who helped to settle him down. He was ridden by Desormeaux in all his races in Y2K and paid $6.60 to win and $4.00 to show. He came out of the #15 hole and broke to the inside, was unhurried, and on the rail, saved ground while advancing on the backstretch, swung out on the final turn seven wide and edged clear under urging and won by one-plus lengths. There were nineteen horses in the race, which made for a big payoff in the exotics.

We sent out a bet by our friend, $20 on the Oaks-Derby Double and bet Secret Status in the Oaks and Fusaichi Pegasus in the Derby. That combination paid $510 on a $20 bet. After Secret Status won the Oaks, we were all jacked up and decided to go all out and bet our usual big show bet plus the exacta, trifecta, and superfecta with various horses; and believe it or not, we cashed every bet we made and collected our biggest payday ever. Bill handled the betting, and when it was over, he proceeded to go through his pockets to find the winning tickets. He could not find the superfecta ($1,635 for a $1 bet), and we were frantic. Finally, it turned up in one of his pockets, and we were relieved. He cashed the tickets, and he sat down on a small cooler we had with us and proceeded to count the wad of money out

in the open on the red bricks of CD. Quickly a crowd gathered, and
I was concerned that someone would grab a fistful of hundred dollars
and run. As he was counting, being inebriated, he fell backward off
the cooler onto the filthy bricks and just kept on counting. He had
just purchased a brand-new sports coat for the occasion. He lay on his
back still counting, and I was trying to guard against theft. It was a
sight to behold, and we still laugh about it to this day. We had finally
hit the jackpot and were eager to even get further smashed. This
stack (cache) would last us for ten more years. His prep races were so
impressive that we had to bet him heavy. Of course we became heady
after that, and we were on top of the world the rest of the year. We
had a few extra swallows after the race.

CHAPTER 16

Monarchos won the 2001 Kentucky Derby on a hot, sunny day and the track was fast. He was owned by John Oxley and trained by John Ward Jr. He was a gray/roan colt sired by Maria's Mon with a Dixlieland Band mare on the distaff and was ridden by J. Chavez. He had won the Florida Derby easily by five lengths and ran second in the Wood Memorial three weeks earlier and had Beyer figures of 105 and 103, respectfully.

Standing at the entrance to the paddock tunnel, we viewed the horses coming and going out of the saddling area. It was a hot day and most of the horses were sweating, but we deduced that the sweat was produced by the heat and not by anxiety or stress. Our system pick was Point Given, a Baffert trained and Stevens mount, and he was sweating, which put us in a quandary as far as appearance was concerned. As we stood there, the horses backed up, and Monarchos stopped right in front of us and was champing at the bit. We knew that was a good sign but ignored it because Point Given and Baffert were such proven winners, and so we bet him and he ran fifth and we lost. Monarchos paid $23 to win. He dropped back early from the sixteenth post and steadily improved his position and went five wide into the far turn and was going away by four lengths. We should have known that lightning wouldn't strike twice in a row, but we ignored the telltale signs and paid dearly for it. We opted for a few drams of 100 proof.

In 2002, War Emblem won the Kentucky Derby on a mostly sunny day and on a fast track. He was owned by Thoroughbred Corporation and trained by Bob Baffert and ridden by Victor

Espinosa. This was the third time in six years that Baffert trained the winner. He had Mr. Prospector (two back) on the top side and a Lord at War mare on the bottom, not necessarily the best, but I would say mediocre. He had previously won the Illinois Derby a month earlier by six lengths. Bob Baffert's group purchased him after that win. This was the first time an Illinois Derby winner at Sportsman Park ever won the Kentucky Derby, as far as I know. He was a front runner and was just coming into his own, this plus a great workout at Churchill Downs pulling up at a mile in 1:39 flat. We somehow missed this tidbit of information much to our chagrin. He had post position #5, a good one; and with his speed, he took the lead from the very start and led all the way around and won by four lengths, going away and paid $43 to win with Proud Citizen the runner-up. The superfecta paid a whopping $91,765, and our pick ran out of the money. We weren't the only ones that got fooled because the *BloodHorse* magazine with Steve Haskin's analysis also stumbled by not picking him even after writing to his favor in his April 24 derby report. He was the champion three-year-old colt. This, however, did not make us feel any better, so we decided to *celebrate*!

Funny Cide won the 2003 Kentucky Derby on a partly sunny day and on a fast track. He was owned by Sackatoga Stable and trained by Barclay Tagg and was a chestnut gelding sired by Distorted Humor and Forty Niner (two back out of the Slewacide mare) with J. Santos in the irons. He won all three of his two-year-old races. He ran second to Empire Maker in the Wood Memorial on a muddy track and had a 110 Beyer figure. He was overlooked in the Kentucky Derby because of Empire Maker's superb back races, and his excellent breeding and was owned by Juddmonte Farms Inc. He had #5 post position and was four wide on the first turn and made his way steadily while improving his position and was second entering the stretch run and won by a couple of lengths on the fast-closing Empire Maker, who ran second under Jerry Bailey. There were sixteen horses in the race, which made for a good betting opportunity. He was the champion three-year-old colt.

Our system picked both Funny Cide and Empire Maker. Funny

Cide paid $27.60 to win, and Empire Maker paid $4.40 to show. Since our system picked both of them in the rankings, we should have bet them in the Exacta, which paid $97.00. In any event, we came out a winner on our show bet on #11 Empire Maker. Bill's wife, Jackie, bet on Funny Cide and was the big winner because she bet exactly what our system revealed. We were satisfied with the result and had one more for the road.

On May 1, 2004, Smarty Jones won the Kentucky Derby on a sloppy track and rainy day. He was owned by Someday Farm and trained by John Servis and ridden by S. Elliot. There were eighteen horses in the race, and he had #13 post even though his saddle cloth was fifteen due to some scratches. He was bred in Pennsylvania (unusual) and sired by Elusive Quality out of I'll Get Along by Smile. He had won both of his starts as a two-year-old on a nondescript track and won his next seven starts, including the Kentucky Derby and Preakness. He ran second in the Belmont Stakes, failing by a length to win the Triple Crown. He had off-track proclivities and won the Arkansas Derby on a muddy track. The sloppy track on May 1 was right to his liking. He paid $10.20 to win and $4.80 to show. He broke from the gate in the fourth position and settled in a good position along the backstretch just behind Lion Hart, closed the gap from the outside midway on the turn, and challenged for the lead at the top of the stretch and wore down Lion Hart to win by about three lengths going away. He was another champion three-year-old colt.

Our system picked the first two finishers, but again, we did not bet the Exacta, which paid $65.20. Our bias again led to our dismay, and I was devastated that we did not bet him on a sloppy track. We did have the Derby Double (Oaks and Derby Winners) paying $62.20, but it wasn't enough to offset our losses. To this day, I still am haunted why we didn't bet Smarty Jones when every statistic pointed to him. Drinks all around!

Giacomo won the 2005 Kentucky Derby on a mostly sunny day on a track listed as fast. He was owned by Mr. and Mrs. Jerome Moss and F. Stronach and trained by John Shirreffs and ridden my Mike Smith. He was sired by Holy Bull out of the Set Them Free, a Stop the Music mare better suited for middle-distance races. He was a gray/roan colt and came out of the #10 post position. He started slow as expected and was five wide on the first turn with twenty horses in the race. He worked his way forward six wide on the far side. He angled out around a wall of horses and closed steadily through the stretch to prevail by half length over Closing Argument and Afleet Alex. He paid a whopping $102.60 to win and the $2.00 superfecta paid box car figures of $1,728,507.50 and an exacta of $9,814.80. The largest I have ever witnessed. Our system pick was Afleet Alex, who ran third, but we did not bet him. *Why?* I don't know. Giacomo ran fourth in the Santa Anita Derby a month earlier with a 95 Beyer rating. We very seldom ever consider a Beyer under 100 to win the Kentucky Derby, but there is always an exception to the rule. The purse had $2,000,000 for the first time, raised from $1,000,000. He did not win another race in 2005. I was in a box near the rail on the first turn with some of my friends from my company days, even though I had retired from corporate America for fourteen years. It was nice to be with them and enjoy a few mint juleps and various alcoholic concoctions.

In 2006, Barbaro won the Kentucky Derby on a beautiful day on a fast track. He was owned by Lael Stables and trained by Michael Matz and ridden by Edgar Prado. He was sired by Dynaformer (Roberto) out of a Carson City mare out of the Raise a Native/ Round Table female family. He was a beautiful brown colt that was undefeated. There were twenty horses in the field, and he had #8 post position. He had won the Florida Derby by five lengths from the outside post position, which solidified our selection and being our #1 pick in our betting system. A crowd of 157,236 attended, second largest in history. This was the second year the Churchill Downs allowed only twenty horses to be entered into the Kentucky Derby. He paid $14.20 to win and $6.00 to show. Bluegrass Cat ran second (longshot) at 30–1, which gave us a big payoff on both ends. Barbaro stumbled at the start and was five wide around the first turn and made his way to the leaders midway in the far turn and reached the lead at the top of the stretch then drew off to win by 6 ½ lengths.

It was a beautiful site to see, especially since we loaded up on him. That made up for our last several losses. He broke down during the Preakness and had to be euthanized eventually. A statue of him was erected at Churchill Downs as a fan favorite.

We were invited to visit Herb's beautiful condo in St. Petersburg, Florida to attend the Tampa Bay Derby, a prep race for the Kentucky Derby, in March, 2007. Believe it or not we won and spent the night in revelry in spite of being in an ethyl alcohol induced semi-comatose condition most of the time.

Street Sense won the Kentucky Derby in 2007. He was owned by James Tafel, trained by Carl Nafzger, and ridden by Calvin Borel. The weather was partly sunny, and the track was fast. He was sired by Machiavellian (Mr. Prospector) out of a Dixieland Band mare and was well suited for the 1 ¼ mile distance. He won the Breeders' Cup Juvenile as a two-year-old by ten lengths at Churchill Downs and was voted the champion two-year-old colt. He was second in the Bluegrass Stakes and was closing fast. We were there at Keeneland to see the race, and we noticed he had plenty left and galloped out very well. He had #7 post position and was reserved at the start and relaxed, reaching the rail before the first turn and settled well in the nineteenth place out of twenty horses. He began picking up horses near the far turn and got through on the inside, and then moved three wide to go after Hard Spun, the leader. He took the lead at the one-eighth pole and continued on resolutely to win by two-plus lengths with Hard Spun running second. He paid $11.80 to win and $4.60 to show. Our system picked them first and second, and that's how they ran. He was nineteenth lengths back at the half-mile mark before rallying to pass fourteen horses for the win. Between our observations, his workout on April 24, 2007, and our system pick we had no reservations on unbuckling our wallets on him. He also won the Travers Stakes in August, and we were in the mood to let the good times roll!

On May 3, 2008, Big Brown won the Kentucky Derby on a partly cloudy day on a fast track. He was owned by IEAH Stables et al., trained by Richard Dutrow Jr., and ridden by Kent Desormeaux.

He was a bay colt sired by Boundary out of a Nureyev mare Mien. There were twenty horses entered and started in the race, and he had #20 post position. This was the first time any horse had won from the extreme outside and caused many punters from not betting him. He was rated off the early pace four wide into the first turn and improved his position in the back stretch and went to the lead at the quarter-pole and increased his lead to win by about five lengths. He paid $6.80 to win and $4.80 to show with the filly Eight Bells running second. When galloping out after the finish line, Eight Bells broke down and had to be put down. She was a great filly, and a hush filled the stands as the jockey jumped down and was trying to hold her leg up to take the weight off. Big Brown won the Florida Derby by six lengths with a 106 Beyer rating. It wasn't hard to pick him from that effort, and he was our system's #1 pick as well, so we bet him and won again. Our confidence was at an all-time high, and we couldn't wait for the next Derby. I had been standing near the same spot in the paddock area for sixty-nine years, and that's where I am going to be as long as I live and can sip my heart medicine, win or lose.

Mine That Bird won the 2009 Kentucky Derby on a cloudy day and on a sloppy track. He was owned by Double Eagle/Buena Suerte, trained by Bennie Wooley Jr. and ridden by Calvin Borel (Bo-Rail) because of his success in the Kentucky Derby by hugging his horse to the rail and saving ground around the oval. There were nineteen horses in the race, and Mine That Bird had post position #8. He broke out of the gate last, continued there along the backstretch, settled in with three furlongs to go, moved with a rush along the inside at the far turn, angled back to the inside with three-sixteenth to go, moved through a small opening, took over in the last one-eighth mile, and drew clear to win by six-plus lengths. The off track suited him to a tee with Birdstone the sire out of a Smart Strike mare. The bay gelding paid $103.20 to win, and we completely overlooked him as did many others. Pioneer of the Nile ran second and paid $6.40 to show, which our system ranked #1 in our analysis. We were able to salvage a few dollars since we bet multiple exotic bets and lost all of them. We vowed not to bet so much on the exotics, but we knew that the payoffs would lure us back in. The trifecta paid $41,500 and the superfecta $557,006. It's hard to pass up taking a chance and then recover our exotic bet losses on our show bets. With 20 horses now eligible to run the combinations are enormous and very difficult to win. Drinks all around!

On May 1, 2010, Super Saver won the Kentucky Derby on a cloudy day and on a sloppy track. He was owned by Win Star Farms LLC, trained by Todd Pletcher, and ridden by Calvin (Bo-Rail) Borel. There were twenty horses in the race, and he came out of the fourth post position. He was sired by Maria's Mon out of Supercharger, an AP Indy mare, and had good off-track proclivities in his back breeding. He broke from the gate in good position, was reserved along the <u>inside</u> and in a good position, moved up after six furlongs, rallied between rivals on the far turn then moved back along the rail, engaged the leader to open a clear lead with an one-eighth of a mile to go, and expanded his lead to win by two-plus lengths. He paid $18 to win and $6 to show. This was Todd Pletcher's first derby win out of the last ten and had been entering two or three horses (a total of twenty-four) for the derby for some time. He was D. Wayne Lucas's protégé, and he had access to the top bred horses of Win Star Farm. This was the third Derby win for Calvin Borel, and he was becoming a celebrity, so to speak, of which he was unaccustomed. A Texan named Glen Fullerton won the CNBC's Derby Dream Bet prize sweepstakes, which gave him $100,000 to bet on the horse of his choice. Believe it to not, he bet it all on Super Saver to win and won $900,000. The superfecta paid $202,569. We split our bet and lost. Our system picked Lookin at Lucky (Baffert's colt) who ran sixth. Our spirits came into play after that blow.

Animal Kingdom won the 2011 Kentucky Derby on a cloudy day and on a fast track. He was owned by Team Valor International, trained by Graham Motion with Johnny Velazquez in the irons. There were nineteen colts in the race, and Animal Kingdom had post position #16. He was a chestnut colt sired by Leroidesanima Rex out of a Dalicia from the Lyphard line, but not prominent in today's lineage. He had won the Spiral Stakes at Turfway on a synthetic track, and most were skeptical whether or not he would take a liking to the Churchill Dirt track. He was reserved for four furloughs, advanced slowly and came out six wide into the stretch, took over in the final furlong, and won by three lengths and paid $43.80 to win. The only person to pick Animal Kingdom was Mike Battaglia, the Churchill Downs Handicapper and morning line maker. His stats improved greatly after this race. He had noticed his outstanding workouts at Churchill Downs the weeks before the derby and saw that he was blossoming out. We lost and did not have a winner or cash-in since Big Brown in 2008 and were somewhat despondent and began to tweak our system again. Ever since some tracks went to the synthetic surface track, our selections had been waning. Tracks like Santa Anita, Keeneland, and Turfway had all went from dirt to synthetic or poly tracks as safety features, which was supposedly more kindly to horses to injuries—an experiment that went sour, and they eventually went back to dirt tracks. Bottoms up!

On May 5, 2012, I'll Have Another won the Kentucky Derby on a partially sunny day, and the track was fast. He was owned by Reddam Racing LLC, trained by Doug O'Neil, and ridden by Mario Gutierrez. There were twenty colts in the race, and he came out of the nineteenth hole. He was a chestnut colt sired by Flower Alley out of an Arch mare, from the back royal lineage and had ran a fast closing race at Santa Anita prior to the derby. He gained a forward position out of the gate and improved his position down the backstretch, came four wide into the stretch, and continued on and drew clear to win by 1 ½ lengths, catching Bodemeister, who had led all the way to the end. He paid $32.60 to win; and Bodemeister, named after Bob Baffert's son, paid $5.60 to show. He also won the Preakness two weeks later and showed promise as a Triple Crown threat. However, that did not come to pass as so many before had tried but failed in the Belmont Stakes. It takes too much out of a horse to win both the derby and Preakness and have fresh horses waiting for you in the Belmont. We made a small bet on Bodemeister, but we were unable to win on the day. It was a tough race to handicap, so we pulled in our horns somewhat and sung the same ole song "Wait

Till Next Year," and so we rationalized our decisions with a couple of short snorts and licked our wounds.

Orb won the 2013 Kentucky Derby on a rainy day and on a sloppy track. He was owned by Stuart Janney III, Phipps Stable, and trained by Claude "Shug" McGaughey III with J. Rosario in the saddle. There were nineteen horses in the race, and Orb had post position #15. He was a bay colt sired by Malibu Moon out of Lady Liberty by Unbridled with good off-track proclivities. He broke from the gate slowly and was angled in and reserved early while four wide on the first turn. He made a bold six wide move commencing near the three-eighth pole; caught the leader, Normandy Invasion, in mid-stretch; and drew clear to win by 2 ½ lengths. He paid $12.80 to win and $5.40 to show with a longshot, Golden Soul, getting up for place that made for a good show price. Our system ranked him #1 as did our other determinants, and we won a considerable amount of greenbacks. He had won his previous three races, including the Florida Derby, and to us was a standout. He was dull for the Preakness two weeks later after he was bet down to an odds-on favorite and finished fourth, some nine lengths off the winner. His previous races had taken its toll, and he did not seem to have the same kind of energy as in the derby. My back and legs were hurting after standing in the paddock for seventy-four years had finally caught up with me, and as always, we eased our physical pain with our favorite drink, Old Redeye, and a tad of water on the rocks.

On May 3, 2014, California Chrome won the Kentucky Derby on a mostly sunny day and on a fast track. He was owned by Steven Coburn and Perry Martin, trained by Art Sherman, and ridden by Victor Espinoza. There were nineteen horses in the race, and he came out of the #5 hole, a good post for his speed. He was a chestnut colt by Lucky Pulpit out of Love the Chase and bred in California. He broke evenly and was three wide at the first turn vying for the lead and challenged, leaving the 5/16 pole and made the lead with a quarter to go. He shook clear and increased his lead and won easily by about two lengths. He paid $7.00 to win and $4.20 to show with a longshot (38–1) running second. That was just what the doctor ordered for us because out system ranked him #1 and had Beyers of 107 and 108 in his previous two races, the San Felipe (GR-2), and the Santa Anita Derby (GR-1). We were at the Tampa Bay downs for the Tampa Bay Derby and saw him on TV win by seven lengths on March 14, and that's when we made up our minds. We cashed in big time and was on a roll. NBC interviewed us before the race because it was my seventy-fifth year attendance of the Kentucky Derby. My granddaughter (Amber Sims) had talked with NBC personnel, and we were surprised when they called. We were interviewed on the veranda next to the gold room overlooking the paddock. They asked me to bring some old memorabilia that I had accumulated over the years, and I brought my 1940 Kentucky Derby program (my first derby). I brought several programs with me, including the 1973 Secretariat program and the one hundredth derby program. Bill also brought some old daily double tickets and others. As we were waiting in line to be interviewed by Carolyn Manno of NBC, the chairman and CEO of Churchill Downs, Robert L. Evans, approached me after his interview and asked me some questions concerning the 1940s pari-mutuel tickets, etc., and gave me his card and asked me to call him so we could chat about the Derby.

Eventually, Carolyn Manno interviewed us, and I showed the camera and viewers my old 1940s Kentucky Derby program. We were expecting some more questions, but the interview was cut short (thirty seconds) for who knows what reason. We got all duded up for the encounter with hats, et al. Later I called Churchill Downs and made an appointment to chat with Mr. Evans. Kim, the senior director of executive administration, gave me a tour of the corporate headquarters, which was quite impressive. Then I met with Mr. Evans, and we have a nice chat about the derby. I had brought with me my large binder with photos of derby winners and all their stats and showed them to him. He was very impressed with my collection. I had saved every ticket, program, and form since 1940. He invited us to be guests of Churchill Downs in 2015. From that day on, we were guests of Churchill Downs each year and gave us a seat due to my aching back and legs to take the load off! They have been very generous to us ever since and just in time to enable me to attend the Kentucky Derby in comfort, and I thank them for that. Up to this time, we (Bob and/or Bill and I) had been standing in the paddock at derby time for a least five hours every year for over fifty years.

Mr. Evans was primarily responsible for all the new renovations at Churchill Downs, modernizing the facility while still keeping the traditional history of the track intact. Today the facility has little resemblance to the track I knew as a boy and man up to the year 2000. It is new, an updated modern facility while still holding some of its traditional ambiance such as the Twin Spires, etc.

To me, the most meaningful innovations was when they went to computerized pari-mutuel betting tickets so you wouldn't have to go to separate windows to buy or cash a ticket, which eliminated the long lines and saved everyone a lot of time and effort. It was a struggle on Derby Day to get your bet up, especially for us, because we had ten or so minutes to bet after we viewed the horses leaving the paddock.

On May 2, 2015, American Pharoah won the Kentucky Derby on a partly cloudy day and on a fast track. He was owned by Zayata Stables LLC, trained by Bob Baffert, and ridden by Victor Espinoza. There were eighteen horses in the race, and he came out of the #15 post position even though his saddle cloth number was eighteen. He was a bay colt sired by Pioneer of the Nile out of Littleprincessemma. He was one to two entries for Bob Baffert, the other one being Dortmund. He broke well and was third at the first turn, in good position behind Dortmund and Firing Line. He sat about a length behind the first two. Around the far turn, American Pharoah began to make his move on the leaders. He caught the leaders at the quarter pole and steadily pulled away to win by a length over Firing Line and Dortmund (third). These were two formidable opponents, and it wasn't a cake walk by any means. He paid $7.80 to win and $4.20 to show, a nice show price considering the odds of the other two finishers. He had previously won the Arkansas Derby by eight lengths with a 107 Beyer rating and had only lost one race. He was our #1 pick, and it was easy to see that he had the makings of a super horse. He looked great in the paddock, and we cashed in big time. He also won the Preakness and the Belmont Stakes and thus became the first Triple Crown winner since Affirmed in 1978 (thirty-seven years ago). He also won the Breeders' Cup Classic later in the year, setting a new track record and was voted the horse of the year. It was drinks all around before and after.

Two weeks prior to the derby we—my wife and I—were interviewed by Connie Leonard of WAVE TV, the local affiliate of NBC, in our home to view my Kentucky Derby memorabilia, which I have been collecting since 1940. The extensive collections included all derby programs; glasses; label pins; photos; statistics of the winners; Triple Crown pari-mutuel tickets of Secretariat, Settle Slew, and Affirmed; and many other artifacts. It was an extensive interview, and she stayed about two hours talking with us. WAVE TV aired it before the derby as a program feature three days before the derby; and also Eric Flack, co-host reporter of Connie and WAVE TV, interviewed Bill and I at the Derby, which was a nice touch for both WAVE TV (Louisville, Kentucky) and us. Since then, I have continued to acquire more memorabilia and have added two more Triple Crown winners, photos, and tickets beautifully framed on our wall with all the others.

Nyquist won the 2016 Kentucky Derby on a mostly cloudy day and on a fast track. He was owned by Reddam Racing LLC, trained by Doug O' Niell, with Mario Gutierrez in the irons. There were twenty horses in the race, and Nyquist had #13 post position. He came out of the gate in good order and was second around the first turn and maintained that position around the far turn before overpowering the leader, Gun Runner, and went on to win by one-plus lengths from the late charging Exaggerator. He was a bay colt sired by Uncle Mo out of a Forestry mare, Seeking Gabrielle, all from excellent back breeding. He paid $6.60 to win and $3.60 to show. He now had eight wins out of eight starts and won the Breeders' Cup Juvenile as a two-year-old. The disappointment that O'Niell had with I'll Have Another soon vanished with this win by Nyquist. He had also won the Florida Derby prior to the Kentucky Derby, and the only question about him was the distance factor of 1 ¼ miles, which now no longer exists. He was an easy pick for us, and our system also ranked him #1 with Exaggerator, who ran second. We were winners once again and had the exacta and just missed the trifecta by a head. This was our fourth straight winner, and our confidence had returned. We were guests of Churchill Downs again, which enabled me to have a comfortable sit-down derby up to the race. This was my seventy-seventh Kentucky Derby, and our alcohol consumption had dwindled considerably.

Always Dreaming won the 2017 Kentucky Derby on a rainy day and on a muddy track on May 6. He was owned by MeB Racing Stables LLC Brooklyn Boys, trained by Todd Pletcher, and ridden by John Velazquez. There were twenty horses in the race, and Always Dreaming came out of the #5 post position. He came out of the gate good to secure a forward position and was second going into the first turn. He raced evenly along the backstretch and took the lead at the ¾ pole and steadily increased his lead to win by two-plus lengths. He was sired by Bodemeister (Empire Maker) out of the Irish mare and had good back breeding. He won his last three starts in 2017 and reached his peak at derby time, including the Florida Derby, on April 1. He paid $11.40 to win and $5.80 to show. He was our system co-pick, along with McCracken, who came out of the #15 hole. The Beyer figures for both were not in the triple digits, and that concerned us, so we were undecided on our choice. As luck would have it, we chose incorrectly and did not win. We were guests of Churchill Down again, and all of our group (eight) had tickets (gate), so at least we didn't have to spend $80/ticket to get into the gate. Fortunately, I again had a seat in the racing office because it rained off and on all day. I left to go to the paddock to see the horses being saddled, etc., and met our group there. The walk back to our car was agonizing for me because my back and legs. Our customary alcoholic consumption was down to one drink. I was eighty-six years old.

On May 5, 2018, Justify won the Kentucky Derby on an extremely rainy day and on a sloppy track. He was owned by China Horse Club, trained by Bob Baffert, and ridden by Mike Smith. There were twenty horses in the race, and Justify came out of the #7 post position. He came out of the gate in good order and fell in behind Promises Fulfilled, the leader. He moved alongside with five furlongs remaining, drew clear at the 3/8 pole, rebuffed the bid of Good Magic near the stretch, continued on resolutely, and won by two-plus lengths. He was sired by Scat Daddy out of a Ghostzapper mare,

Stage Magic. He had both speed and stamina on both the top and bottom sides in his breeding. This was Bob Baffert's fifth derby win and second time behind Ben Jones, who trained for Calumet back in the '40s. More than 157,000 fans attended this derby in spite of the all-day rain. He paid $7.80 to win and $4.40 to show, and the exacta paid $69.60. It was the wettest Kentucky Derby in the history of the race and was only one of two horses that won the race after not raced as a two-year-old. He went on to win the Preakness and the Belmont Stakes, and thus became the thirteenth Triple Crown Winner, two in the last four years. Again, Churchill Down furnished us tickets, and I was again in the racing office and out of the rain, but I went out to the paddock as usual to view the contenders. We bet heavily on him and reaped a nice reward. He won all six of his races and retired undefeated after the Belmont Stakes. His Triple Crown digit Beyer ratings were enough to impress us and our system ranked him #1. It was an easy choice for us and was the ninth Triple Crown winner that I had witnessed in my seventy-nine Kentucky Derby attendances. This was a special day all the way around in spite of the weather, and kudos to Churchill Downs for enabling me to be comfortable for this eventful day. He was a super horse. One drink was all we could handle.

Country House won the 2019 Kentucky Derby on a showery day and on a sloppy track. He was owned by J. V. Shields Jr. and Mrs. J. V. McFadden Jr., trained by Bill Mott and ridden by Flavien Prat. He was sired by Lookin at Lucky out of a War Chant mare with excellent back breeding. Lookin at Lucky was the first horse in more than three decades to win the Eclipse Award at both ages two and three. Country House was placed first after only the second disqualification in Derby History. The Stewards declared that the first place finisher, Maximum Security, had committed a foul at the top of the stretch by veering over into the path of the other horse slightly behind him and had endangered all the other horses and jockeys. The three Stewards deliberated for about fifteen minutes before disqualifying Maximum Security, and a controversy ensued. Most thought that the interference by Maximum Security did not warrant being disqualified, especially in the Kentucky Derby. It's the writer's opinion that the Stewards did the right thing. Country House had post position #18 and settled in the middle of the pack into the first turn and loomed boldly outside Maximum Security near the 1/8 pole and was not affected by the leader and finished two-plus lengths behind Maximum Security. This was Bill Mott's first Derby win, and the outcome will be discussed for years to come. Our system had ranked Omaha Beach #1 and Improbable next. We bet Improbable because Omaha Beach was scratched the day before the derby with an epiglottis problem that affected his breathing. The winner paid a whopping $132.10 to win, but we didn't cash a ticket on this derby. We were again guests of Churchill Downs, and I was interviewed by NBC since this was my eightieth derby. NBC interviewed me in the racing office, and it took three takes before they were satisfied. Each time I had to come up with a different vocal because I had forgotten what I had said in the previous two. The whole thing took about fifteen minutes, and it was shown on TV for about thirty seconds. A lot of hullabaloo about very little air time. I hope this is my last interview because it was an ordeal!

CHAPTER 17

In 2020, the Kentucky Derby was delayed from May 2 until September 5 (my daughter's birthday) because of a global pandemic of the coronavirus and most of the sporting events were either delayed or cancelled. The virus entered the USA in late January and is still continuing to spread into 2021 and will probably do so for some time to come.

In any event, the derby was scheduled for September 5, and a prep race was inserted for the actual Derby Day on May 2 (Arkansas Derby), and the Belmont Stakes was run as the first race in the Triple Crown on June 20 at 1 1/8 miles in distance in lieu of 1 ½ miles.

In the interim between the Belmont and the Kentucky Derby, the Travers Stakes (the summer derby) was run on August 20 at 1 ¼ mile, and the same colt won both races (Tiz the Law) convincingly and was a heavy odds-on favorite to win the derby. All these races were run without fans in attendance due to the contagious virus. All sports were changed to some degree, and the 2020 Olympic games in Japan were also cancelled, hopefully to occur in 2021.

Authentic won the Kentucky Derby for Spendthrift Farms and Others and again Bob Baffert was the trainer; his sixth Kentucky Derby won, which tied him with Ben A. Jones of Calumet Farms in the '40s and '50s and was ridden by J. R. Velazquez. There were eighteen horses entered, and three were scratched. So a fifteen-horse field lined up in the new twenty-horse starting gate for the Run for the Roses on a beautiful sunny day with approximately one thousand onlookers in the cavernous stands of Churchill Downs. Two of those in attendance were Bill and myself due to the generosity of Churchill

Downs on my behalf because of my attendance of now eighty-two years. I want to thank them and especially Kim (Senior Director of Executive Administration), a truly beautiful and efficient young lady who had enabled me to attend the derby in comfort for the last five years.

Also, at this time, protests for police brutality were taking place all over the country, especially in Louisville, after a black woman was killed in a no-knock warrant arrest. The protests have been on-going for several months, and they vowed to prevent the running of the Kentucky Derby. They marched and surrounded the track but did not resort to violent tactics, and there were no problems to speak of. Kim arranged for us to have perfect seats near the finish line, and we enjoyed ourselves immensely.

Authentic was #18 and in the outside post position. He got out of the gate on top and led all the way around the oval. Tiz the Law, the 3–5 favorite tried to reel him in entering the stretch, but could not catch the superbly fit winner and ran second and paid $3.40 to place and $3.20 to show. We bet him again heavily to show and came out winners again. The winner, Authentic, paid $18.80 to win and only $5.00 to show. Mr. Big News ran third at 46–1, which helped our show price. The Preakness in 2020 was the third leg of the Triple Crown.

This was a momentous occasion for Bill and I because only less than one thousand people witnessed the race in person at the track. Earlier (two weeks), I was interviewed by NBC concerning my derby longevity and also at the track on Derby Day, which was broadcast nationally. Also, I was interviewed by others over the telephone and was quoted in the Churchill Downs Oaks and Derby Day programs, as well as the Churchill Downs magazine, which was a pleasant surprise for me, even though it was an ordeal at my age to respond to these in-depth interviews. Never in my dreams did I think that a fun thing for me over the years would turn into this kind of notoriety, and thusly became one of the most momentous of all the eighty-two derbies that I had attended.

On Friday (Oaks Day), I received a call from a local newspaper reporter asking me to call a man from Columbus, Ohio, about attending the derby. He apparently was looking for some notoriety, saying that he invited me to view the derby from outside the racetrack, thinking I would not be allowed inside the track. He had come up with a scheme to view the derby from about half a mile away via a scissor forklift on a VFW Post property across the street from the track. He had hired a truck and lift to view the derby and wanted me to accompany him and his entourage. At first, I thought it was a joke. I politely refused because I was to see the Kentucky Derby from the best seats in the house, thanks to Churchill Downs. We saw the lift from our seats for a while, but did not see it at derby time. I still wonder what happened. To me it was a very weird request and was beyond my comprehension.

Churchill Down – Kentucky Derby – 2020
(Limited Attendance due to Corona Virus – COVID-19 Pandemic)

Bill & John – Kentucky Derby – 2020 – Limited attendance
due to Corona Virus – COVID 19 Pandemic.

Being able to attend the 2020 derby has made me more aware of the unique situation that I am in and gives me added impetus to keep this streak alive. I never once entertained the thought of this accomplishment for the first fifty years, and I took for granted that attending the derby was a matter of fact that I enjoyed, and that urge satisfied my gambling instinct, my competitive nature to win and the need to <u>not</u> lose money that I could not afford, especially with a family to support during the hard times for us in the '40s and '50s. Three children in thirty-five months dictated a frugal lifestyle, and if not for my wife (Doris), I could not have been able to achieve this milestone. So many situations like this occurred over the years that it almost seems to me that somehow destiny was a factor that contributed to me being willing and able to keep this streak alive. It seems unreal that I have escaped all the pitfalls that come with life's trials and tribulations to obtain this feat.

On May 1, 2021, Medina Spirit won the Kentucky Derby on a

beautiful sunny say with the temperature in the seventies and on a fast track. He is owned by Zedan Racing Stables and trained by Bob Baffert and ridden by J. R. Velazquez. Bob's seventh derby win, a record, and second in a row for J. R.

Medina Spirit came out of the #8 post position. He broke very well and assumed the lead at the first turn followed by eighteen other colts. He maintained his lead all the way and turned back several challengers throughout and won by about half a length. He paid $26.20 to win, $12.00 to place, and $7.60 to show. The favorite was Essential Quality, who ran fourth. Mandaloun was second and paid $23.00. Hot Rod Charlie paid $5.20 to show. We bet the favorite to show and lost our show bet by a head. Such is life when betting on horse racing! Incidentally, a bedding/mattress owner by the name of James Mackingvale (Mattress Mack) bet $2,000,000 on Essential Quality to win, which reduced his odds somewhat. He apparently is a big better on lots of sporting events. He made his bet public for whatever reason, and that is the first time I ever heard that someone went public with that kind of bet, apparently a publicity stunt or tax implication.

Unfortunately, the winner, Medina Spirit was disqualified by Churchill Downs after a lab test turned up an illegal substance in his system. The substance was betamethasone and was applied to the colt's hind leg as an ointment for a skin ailment. This substance was banned regardless of what it was used for, and Churchill Downs had no other choice than to disqualify him. The NYRA banned the trainer from running his horses in New York tracks this season. A hearing by Kentucky Racing Commission has not been held as of this writing. They will determine whether or not to officially disqualify Medina Spirit.

However, he was allowed to run Medina Spirit in the Preakness in Baltimore, Maryland, and he ran third. Since the disqualification was after the fact, the betters did not lose their payoffs on Medina Sprit. This happened one other time in 1968 when Dancer's Image was disqualified after winning the derby. The owners will have to return the winning purse money and trophy and award to Mandaloun, the new winner. Because of the illegal substance used, the trainer of Medina Spirit, Bob Baffert, was suspended from racing at Churchill Downs, or any of its affiliates, for two years, ending after the spring meet of 2023.

The attendance was about fifty-two thousand, about one-third of the regular attendance, because of the coronavirus pandemic restrictions. We—Bill and I—were again guests of Churchill Downs, and they furnished us box seats with all the amenities to boot. This was perpetrated by our contact, the vivacious Kim, who has done so for the last six years. We lost and did not cash a ticket on the derby. We did not celebrate with our usual alcoholic intake, but did have a couple of beers before we ate, which <u>now</u> was more than enough to drown our disappointment.

It's rather ironic that, as unconcerned and unpretentious as I was about most things, this notoriety has come to me because I did not seek it or necessarily want it. This state-of-mind also followed me into the corporate world for I did not seek to be promoted beyond the managerial level. I was satisfied with a mid-management position, but alas, I was promoted to VP, and those last years as an executive left a bad taste in my mouth due to inept bosses who were outsiders brought in to eliminate long-time serving workers, which I refused to do.

What started out as an eight year old child's desire, then an interest to satisfy a whim, then an excuse not to apply fully an academic pursuit, and then a life-changing accident event that gave me time to evaluate my chances of success and decide what a male of my persuasion might do in order to live a fruitful and happy life, led to a life of many extraordinary pursuits and adventures that was completely unexpected. At work, I teamed with my boss to research a statistical endeavor of past races at Churchill Downs at the main public library for two years and assembled enough data and a sample size in order to determine if certain ways to bet was viable. I gained a substantial amount of knowledge from this undertaking and was well worth the time and effort. This, with my previous knowledge, has enabled me <u>not</u> lose money by betting race horses through the years and betting only certain races that were predictable. You cannot beat the races by betting every single race, but you must be selective as to which race will be more likely to give you a better chance of winning. The Kentucky Derby, with a large number of horses to choose from, has become my primary focus because the ROI is greater for us, and we have concocted an objective statistical system to assist us in our betting decisions. Since that time, thoroughbred racing has become my passion and has been an asset to me at work and play.

My Kentucky Derby experiences and accounts are now up to date and have taken me down memory lane in reliving these bygone cherished episodes and the great times with my wife, father, mother, and buddies over these many years at the track and after the race. Also, many hours I spent with my parents in their house studying the racing form and analyzing who to bet on. In the early days of my youth, my father would purchase a racing form at the Liberty New Stand in Downtown Louisville late (10:00 p.m.) Friday night before the Saturday races.

We would all gather at his house Saturday afternoon to take turns reading the form and deciding on who and where we were going to bet our $0.50 and $1.00 parlays. In the 1950s, the racing form only cost fifty cents. My father, with his vast knowledge of thoroughbred horses, would mark on the form as to which horses he considered to be contenders on Saturday morning, which was very helpful to all who were present, sometimes up to six to eight people. As a young man, it was a glorious time for me with all the activities that were happening. Others would bring whiskey, beer, or whatever to imbibe during the course of the afternoon, and we bet conservatively through our bookies, one of which was on almost every corner or thereabouts. I learned everything I now know from these get-togethers, and it served me well through the years. A little illegal betting was enjoyed by all.

I think my father's hidden agenda was to use these festivities to kick off his weekend drinking forays to soothe his anxieties. Of course, when the races were in town, we were in attendance at Churchill Downs and Keeneland after I was mustered out of the army. How I found time to participate in all the extracurricular activities while raising a family boggles my mind. My energy and constitution allowed me to do many things through the years, some good and some dumb. Now at my age, I can hardly fathom the drive I had, and for what reason? All on a shoestring financial condition.

I started smoking when I was fifteen and quit when I was sixty. I started drinking alcohol at eighteen and I essentially quit when I was eighty-eight, but started tapering when I was eighty. This is usually a death sentence, but I guess my gene pool and intrinsic characteristics saved my butt up to now anyways. I've had five automobile wrecks, four of which were life-threatening. Three of these were multiple rollovers, two in civilian life and one in a Jeep in the army (roll bar up), and totaled two cars—another ironic twist of favorable fate. How lucky can one person be? I thank God every day for the good fortune he has bestowed on me. If not for my ancestors and wife of sixty-seven years, I would have been gone and forgotten and could not have the many Kentucky Derbies to show for my escapades.

There have been many changes to thoroughbred racing since 1940, and I've had to adapt to them as far as wagering and other safety features that have been enacted. Since Matt Winn made Kentucky Derby famous, he introduced many innovative changes that helped to make Churchill Downs and the Kentucky Derby a global name. Among other things, he introduced $2 pari-mutuel betting so that the masses might better indulge in this pastime. I think he can be considered the person that put the derby on the map. Unfortunately, he passed away in 1949, but he left his mark on the derby behind. He fashioned the Kentucky Derby after the English derby at Epsom Downs, and translated even more than its counterpart in today's world.

Other changes have been made in what medications can be administered to the horses before and on the day of the race. Lasix was introduced in Maryland in 1974 and lastly in New York in 1995. Lasix is described as an anti-bleeding medication used by veterinarians to prevent respiratory bleeding in horses running at high speeds. Lasix and many other illegal drugs are performance enhancing. Due to injuries to horses lately (2019) and other factors, Lasix is now a controversial medication to be used the day the horses race, and Churchill Downs has stated, "It is our intention to run the 2021 Kentucky Derby without … Lasix."

The racing industry has grown considerably since I was a boy, and it is now a multibillion-dollar industry, led by big spenders and sheiks who spend as much as 10-million-plus dollars on one yearling at the Keeneland sales. Other participants are made up of syndicates of many people because of the expense of raising and training a horse. We were members of a small syndicate back in the '80s and '90s, but the ROI on that investment was a minus, so we fell out of the syndicated group. Now we just stick to betting and having fun to satisfy out primal instinct to gamble on something. Once I am at the race track, I forget all my trials and tribulations, and I concentrate on trying to win a few bucks.

The other big change to betting is the ways in which you can place a wager at the track or OTB (off-track betting). The exotic wagering has added millions of dollars for the race track and the states (taxes) that are extracted from each bet made. This take, or vic, had reached about 20 percent on all wagers, and just like in Vegas, the house always comes out on top. The punter has to overcome this take out, which is almost impossible. That is why we bet to show on Derby Day and bet small amounts on other days. If you are a competitor, then wagering on horses is a good mental exercise because you are actually competing against your fellow betters. And since most everyone thinks they are smarter than the other guy, it makes a body feel good when you (so-called) outsmart the other punters. Har har!

The racing industry must have strict regulations on medications in order for it to survive. Other sports, such as football, basketball, soccer, baseball, etc., have taken over by non-participating member of the public. The age of electronics has taken its toll on horse racing. When you can sit on the couch or gaze at your iPhone, etc., it's much easier to do because it requires very little effort. The younger people are all about emails, texting, googling, tweeting, and selfies rather than participating, other than attending loud mind-blowing concerts of various music and videos.

The horse racing industry is slowing losing its appeal to the general public, and any illegal or off-handed dealings, which are present in all sports, must be regulated; and those who flirt with breaking the rules must be reprimanded so that the perception of the public is not detrimental. It appears the past time of the American public is non-participatory since you can watch almost anything to do with professional or amateur sports on TV or mobile device. I, too, have fallen into this habit of watching rather than doing. The public demands that sports be honest and above suspicion of graft of all kinds, such as kickbacks, illegal subsidies, etc., be investigated to keep the attention of the viewers.

The Kentucky Derby, among other races, especially instrumental in offering a fair and legal operation of the sport to retain its followers and attract new participants. Very few sport endeavors offer the kind of moral support and fair play. This is one reason that I have kept alive my enthusiasm for the Kentucky Derby for all these years.

There are numerous pastimes and/or hobbies that one can engage in, and most of them take money and require some effort. I would say or estimate that the one I chose to participate in constitutes about 5 percent of the population or less. In order to have chosen this part time, you had to be schooled in it at an early age, and you had to be of a conservative nature and very frugal with your money management. I happen to fall into both of these categories and thusly became my passion. I, of course, had no idea or inkling that I would have ended up as the only person on the planet to have attended the Kentucky Derby for eighty-two years. In addition, I have been present in the paddock over those years when the horses were saddled and the call for riders up was uttered. As I now look back on it all, it has been a privilege for me to have experienced such an iconic event for so long. To think of the deterrents and stymies that I encountered along the way, some as I have indicated earlier, it defies the probability of logical thought process, and I was extremely lucky to have survived life and death, much less reach this milestone that involves the oldest continuous sporting event in the USA. It used to be called the Sport of Kings because only the well-to-do could participate in it.

Over the years, the popularity of thoroughbred racing has waxed and waned. I think we are now experiencing the waning of this endeavor due to the proliferation of smart phones, media coverage of all sports, social media, and so on.

If not for my grandfather (a blacksmith, among other things) and my father's knowledge of the sport, I would not have had the opportunity to accomplish this unheard-of biographical achievement. It used to be in the '50s and '60s that golf was the primary pastime to further relationships with vendors, etc., but I changed that in my situation to make the Kentucky Derby my primary attribute in establishing good relations with our many suppliers and, in fact, persuaded our primary vendor to again reduce the cost of their products significantly at the Kentucky Derby in 1987, which has never been done before or after my tenure as VP of purchasing. I may be repeating myself, but to be unique in two categories is worth iterating again.

While unwillingly listening to my father pontificate about the horses and many other things, I never once thought that this sleep deprivation would somehow become beneficial to me later in life. One of his favorite modern-day songs was "Que Sera, Sera (Whatever Will Be, Will Be)." Another enduring quality he had was listening to operas with the great tenors Enrico Caruso and Galli Curci, who were the greatest tenors and sopranos of his era. He played the "Sextet from Lucia" most of the nights and on weekends turned it up to the highest volume on the portable record player and tried purposely to wake the neighbors. The police were called many times, and when they came, he talked them into listening also, but at a lower volume. He scoffed at Bing Crosby, Frank Sinatra, and others, saying their voices had no volume. Anyway, I learned a lot but disregarded it as asinine when I was a boy. I'm quite sure that he learned his love of opera from his mother, who had a love of the fine arts that she acquired as a student at St. Catherine's College in Louisville, Kentucky. My grandfather and grandmother proved that opposites attract. As we go down life's highway, we live and learn. Back to racing …

Everyone knows that beating the race horse game is an exercise in futility, but beating a particular race is possible, and the Kentucky Derby has been my savior in this regard. My aggressive gambling nature was tempered by my father's conservative betting strategy, which allowed man's gambling instincts to be satisfied without being a liability. This has been my modus operandi over the years and allowed me to pursue a hobby that kept my mind busy and potentially out of trouble.

Many so-called experts of thoroughbred horse racing think they have more insight and knowledge than the next guy, and surely, they somehow have acquired this know-how without working in the industry, and this is evident concerning the Kentucky Derby. Since we are actually betting against each other, I feel I have an advantage at the derby. All I can say is that I stand by my credentials and experience; what do the experts stand on? *The Kentucky Derby, that's what it's all about!*

A charmed life is not without its setbacks and tragedies, and on February 16, 2021, we experienced the worst calamity that we could have imagined when our youngest son, Thomas, passed away as a result of an accidental fall down his apartment steps (thirteen) on or about January 10, 2021. He was sixty-one years of age and had been disabled from a previous fall from a three-hundred-foot cliff in 1978, as mentioned previously. As I stated earlier, it was a miracle that he survived this long and led a spartan hard life since that time.

His mother and sister assisted him religiously over the next forty-two-plus years. He was able to maintain living independently with their help over the ensuing years under trying circumstances that I could not have endured.

A tribute to him at his funeral ceremony was read by his nephew, Brandon Sims, and is attached in the following pages.

We cannot express our grief here, but this occurrence has been a heart-wrenching one that we will never forget, and I did not expect this to occur before my passing. As a child and young man, his attributes were way beyond mine as we worked together to improve ourselves. The fickle finger of fate stepped in to the raise its ambiguous head in this case. The worst incident of my life. Note that the photos of the kin that were mentioned in the manuscript are opposite the bios of them in the back of the book.

A Tribute to Tom
August 12, 1959 – February 16, 2021

Tom was a pleasant unassuming person with a fun-loving attitude and was very humble in his achievements until he met with a near-death accident when we was nineteen, in the prime of his life. He fell from a three-hundred-foot cliff on a holiday and miraculously survived, but not without serious repercussions.

A brain stem injury left him with a loss of memory, but he rehabilitated himself over a period of time to regain his physical strength through long aerobic walks, sometimes up to ten miles. His determination and perseverance permitted him to live independently, so to speak.

His loving mother devoted forty-plus years to assist him in this endeavor to relieve his frustrations of not fulfilling his dreams and ambitions, later his caring sister also assisted in this difficult task.

He still retained his pleasant personality when with others, and they (mother and father) spent many hours talking and laughing about happenings that occurred before his fateful life-changing event.

Thomas, we salute you today for enduring a spartan life for many years, and you are our hero and inspiration to carry on under adverse circumstances.

You'll always be remembered as our soul man.

CHAPTER 18

Pontification

Some survivors of traumatic events are, in a way, a blessing in disguise. You find growth in some areas, like personal strength, and a different perspective on life and spirituality. Some become more aware of life's fragility, and while it is detrimental to some, others become more focused. This paradox can go either way, and the positive effect is more resilience, adaptability, and coping skills.

Those who put others down as a way to lift themselves is self-serving of course, and they don't realize that others can see right through this play. People who boast about themselves don't even recognize the full extent of the negative response. A self-proclaimed awesomeness with a huge ego is human frailties that others find loathsome.

Sometimes we overvalue the advice of credentialed experts while undervaluing the input of regular people. A cognitive quirk called optimism bias hoping that things will work out even though the odds are against you. Most of us have a cognitive blind spot called egocentric bias, which means that we put more stock in our own opinion than from opinions of others, which can lead to wrong decisions.

Both my liberal and scientific education played a big role in my career. I will point out here that the quality control lab was initiated in 1956 to get to the bottom of line problems. Constant stoppage of the lines were accented by finger-pointing at each other for the causation of these problems. When I became manager of the lab,

I had to analyze and correct, if possible, each breakdown. This required an unbiased opinion based on facts alone, which I have been trained on in <u>spades</u>.

I couldn't have cared less who got pissed off at my written reports, but my writing skills and presentation were excellent, as I was told, but I know it anyway. Har har! After so many years, I was able to get to the crux of the problem most of the time. I spent a lot of time and effort observing the line functions day by day, and I enjoyed my job because it left me alone with minimal supervision.

I also feel that I have the ability to disregard impertinent information that is often misleading and concentrate only on logical coherent info and zero in on real truth and come to a real solution rather than being sidetracked and going down the wrong path. This has enabled me to solve many root problems that may arise almost every day of our existence and avoid the consequences of false assumptions. As you can plainly determine, I have joined the me, myself, and I generation after seventy-five years of actually minimizing my <u>so-called</u> attributes. In fact, I've actually downplayed any assets that I may have had in order to gain insight to the hidden agendas of others and give them a false set of confidence, and if adhered to, can lead to them eating some humble pie, which most of us need from time to time. However, most of those that are proved wrong usually rationalize and justify it and cannot <u>admit</u> they are <u>wrong</u>.

I had always been an action person rather than a talking head, and I get bored easily with idle, meaningless chatter; and it pains me to pretend to be interested in what someone had for dinner or whatever.

My dear sister Jo-Ann was a whiz-bang social person who could charm anyone; she was a social giant and was very successful in being liked because she complemented everyone and all wanted to be around her, especially at social gatherings and parties.

It's amazing that we both had different personas coming from the same household. She chose one path to succeed, and I chose another in order to combat the emotional roller coaster of our young lives. I wrote her a poem on her seventieth birthday outlining a short version of her life, which is included in the back of this anthology.

My younger brother Richard faced different circumstances than my sister and I. By the time he was in high school, we both were gone from home. My sister got married, and I was in college and the US Army. Since he primarily depended on me, I think he felt abandoned and didn't obtain the confidence he might have had. As stated earlier, he had a severe emotional breakdown while I was in the service and he was in his senior year of high school. When I returned from my hitch in the army, I hardly knew him, and it broke my heart. I really never got over it even though I never talked about it. My father, to his credit, did everything he could to try to make his life tolerable.

So far, I have experienced five close calls with death due to a reckless bulletproof attitude, and I consider that a minor miracle. Along with other foolish escapades, I consider myself a very <u>lucky</u> person to still be alive. That, in part, is why I have undertaken this writing so that my descendants will learn not to act on impulse, but rather to think things through and be aware of the consequences of foolish behavior. Most people say they would like to go back and relive their earlier years, but not I, because I believe that I would never make it in the second time around. I still wake up in a cold sweat with bulging eyeballs dreaming of some of the harrowing incidents that I somehow escaped.

My early childhood ordeals and close calls with disaster are not that unusual, but that and the fact that I was fortunate enough to have attended the Kentucky Derby for eighty-two years make me unique in that no one else on earth had achieved this milestone. Whether or not this autobiography is historical remains to be judged by others as noteworthy is important or not, as yet will be determined. As long as my descendants think so, then I will have succeeded in my mission to leave a legacy they can build on or abandon. I've decided at this age that I'm going to be the egotistical dude that I really wasn't. I have to keep up with the times. Amen!

My father often iterated that there is no limit what some people might do and then attempt to try and justify the deed. "Who knows what evil lurks in the hearts of men! Who knows? The shadow knows!"

There are a hundred different definitions of smart, so I won't attempt to define it, but rather prefer to make insight my choice of a beneficial traits. There is no substitute for brains, as he often said. When inebriated, he often sang songs that were indicative of his beliefs, like "Don't Let the Stars Get in Your Eyes," a Perry Como hit, and "Que Sera, Sera (Whatever Will Be, Will Be)."

I learned as a boy from my father in all-night sessions that put me way ahead of my peers. Because of that, I had the insight to see through the veiled masquerade that some portray. The song "I Go to Church on a Sunday Just to Show that I'm an Honest Man" sums up the hidden agenda that most of us have. "Oh, what a tangled web we weave, when first we practice to deceive." It is my intention overall to make this bio. *We*-oriented rather than a *me*-oriented diatribe.

Some other musings that I have are as follows:

- If I tell somebody everything that I know, then combined with everything they know, they will know more than I know!
- It's not what you earn, it's what you keep.
- My hidden agenda is exposing those who have a disparaging hidden agenda.
- "For every action, there is an equal and opposite reaction."

As mentioned earlier and bears repeating, in my day and before, we carried our bourbon on our hips; today they carry their guns on their hips and it has become a sad situation. Any disagreement among people can become a shooting instead of a fist fight or such. I didn't think I would live to see this day come, but it's here now, because everyone expresses their stupid opinions, which is primarily spread through social media, such as Twitter, Instagram, TikTok, etc.; and the freedom of speech amendment (first in the Bill of Rights) from which it has digressed and which was not intended to be.

Before I conclude this autobiography/anthology, I would be remiss not to mention the most influential person in my life. My mother, of course, was the one person I most wanted to please and make happy. She persevered through verbal and emotional abuse that I referenced earlier and refused to acquiesce to any form of intimidation or hardship that came her way. She had an indomitable spirit that was not to be denied. Her father, Joseph M. Roby, and mother, Annie Bean, passed on early; and she, as the oldest girl, took over after her mother died in childbirth while she was nine to ten years old. Her father passed on about ten years later. She had three bothers and one sister. They resided on a small farm near Bardstown, Kentucky, and her father was a prominent politician in that area. She attended Nazareth near Bardstown, and when her father passed on, she came to Louisville to attend nursing school at St. Mary and Elizabeth Hospital and was awarded her RN with four others in the early 1920s.

She always inspired me to take the bull by the horns and do something with my life that was constructive and to always be kind and considerate of those less fortunate than I. I did not want to attend college, but I knew that was what she wanted. Somehow, I was able to accomplish her wishes, and that made her proud and happy. Finally, I had done something right because that was what she was all about. She was the backbone of our family. On her seventieth birthday, I wrote her a poem/verse that highlighted her life, and that was my first attempt at iterating a legacy through verse. I had it framed, and it hung on her wall until she died at ninety-two years of age. Her legacy is revealed in a brief synopsis in the back on this anthology. All my father's siblings (eight) were skeptical people, while my mother's siblings (four) were more trusting and accommodating, and I have a smattering of both of these traits. I have a tendency to be skeptical, while my wife, Doris, tends toward a trusting nature.

There are many more incidents and situations that I don't care to elaborate on and will leave those misdemeanors to someone else to tell, but hopefully those tales will remain unsaid. I plead not guilty to whatever my adversaries accuse me of, and I'm counting on my few dear friends to defend my escapades on the grounds of insanity.

"Forgive them for they know not what they do" applies to most wild and senseless male activities.

I recite the Lord's Prayer frequently, inasmuch as "forgive us our trespasses and forgive those who trespass against us." I try to follow this train of thought, and I haven't any scores to settle. My DNA prevents me from total forgiveness and provides an incentive and motivation for me to keep on trucking. I will not admit to any indiscretion, and I plead the fifth if challenged.

That's what I am all about, and I now declare myself an advocate of the me-me group of GOAT (greatest of all time) after eighty years of listening to others proclaim their assets and people of my ilk enduring others that brag about their so-called accomplishments. It's time to join the egotistical mentality of the twenty-first century, while they did nothing to build this country to what it was and still is for <u>now</u>!

I urge those of our clan to be continuous and don't make any rash decisions or judgments and be aware of the consequences of any action that they may undertake in order to avoid a mistake that can't be undone. As my father would say, "Sleep on it," and ask an older, experienced person for their opinion.

We, the people, are slowly becoming a nation of not admitting we have made mistakes, but rationalizing them by making excuses for every boo-boo we've made. All of us have made errors in judgment one time or another, but for God's sake, cowboy up and admit it.

I realize that many others have overcome some dire circumstances to achieve their goals and aspirations, and I certainly respect them for overcoming whatever cards that they were dealt. My situation does not compare in the hardships category, but it was unique and unusual and fostered perseverance to do my own thing and not follow the leader, so to speak.

As I stated previously, I was able to deal with a gambling instinct by being prudent with my resources and never betting my last dollar. We all know you can't beat the house or the races, but you can beat <u>a</u> race if you do your research and bet light on the losers.

I would like to say here that I consider myself no better or worse than anyone else on this planet, but rather a persistent, lucky guy to have had the opportunity to be free to do what I wanted to do unencumbered by the beliefs and prejudices that exist. The obstacles that I faced early on became a driving force and impetus behind my small successes.

They say it's mind over matter, but if you don't <u>mind</u>, it don't <u>matter</u>. It's is my intention to leave a legacy for those who follow, a stick-with-it attitude, and that's what matters.

The quiet confidence that I had early on was somewhat tempered as I pursued my education; meaning that I was a lot more cautious in my deliberations of the ensuing consequences of rash judgments and actions. I suppose the best example of my behavior is depicted in the classic song "The Gambler," which says "You gotta know when to hold 'em, you gotta know when to fold 'em. You gotta know when to walk away and know when to run." My persona had long been formed before this informative song was written, and a number of variables, some listed in this bio, was responsible for my demeanor. Let's just say that I wasn't lacking self-esteem. I hope this is not taken as bragging, but actually, it is an inescapable fact as I am not about to be bashful in the regard since I think these traits can help in keeping my descendants out of unnecessary trouble. This type of attitude has to be developed, and if you have a proclivity toward gambling, it is absolutely essential that this philosophy be practiced if you want to survive the dark side of gambling. Other quite unbecoming traits are many, but the one that I was most obsessed with is getting even, which is now waning.

If someone undermines me or my immediate kin, I am inclined to return the favor in kind no matter how long it takes to respond. I always pay every debt I owe. Thank God I don't have any more debts to pay, because justice has been consummated for the misdeeds against my own. A day of reckoning will come for those that mistreat an underprivileged person. A remarkable reminder that looking back, as I am doing, is a good motivation for moving forward. Learning from your or others' mistakes can be very beneficial for those that want to learn. Sometimes truth is stranger than fiction. I refuse to accept the inevitable without leaving some kind of mark or footprint behind for those of my clan, especially since I am the last person in this former family that is still alive to tell this story.

That spectacular end-over-end wreck that I had when I was nineteen in 1950 with my future wife in the car was beyond believable, and if it had been filmed, it would have made the top 10 of all time; it was a highlight reel. We ended up 100 yards into a corn field upside down, with the wheels up and the radio still playing. I kicked out the driver's side window to escape. Both of us survived; that in itself was a miracle. Cars of today would not have withstood such a pummeling. That was my second big mistake, and I still have nightmares of the potential consequences of my actions. I was in two more turnover wrecks, but I wasn't driving. There were *no* seat belts or airbags in those days, and I wasn't hurt in any of them. Fortunately, none of them were sudden stops. I am still alive by the grace of God, and I won't reveal any more of my improprieties in this autobiography.

The episodes iterated in this autobiography only scratched the surface of other interesting instances that occurred over a long, fruitful ninety years. I have so many unbelievable stories, and if my health holds out, I may reveal the rest of the story in the future. For me and the Kentucky Derby horses, it is post time.

I'll leave the reader with some original thoughts:

There <u>ain't</u> no cure for my disease of love for the Kentucky Derby and gambling. The thought of the next derby is what keeps me alive.

- My hidden agenda is exposing those who have a disparaging hidden agenda.
- They don't know what they don't know.
- Leadership is not talking and scheming, but rather what actions you take and not being a yes-man.
- My childhood environment was conducive to late hours, gambling, and insight of human frailties.
- There are many different definitions of <u>smart,</u> so I won't attempt to define it, but rather prefer to make <u>insights</u> my choice.

- The roots of my inheritance run deep, and my intention here is to pass it along for whatever its worth.

Here are some quotes and thoughts to ponder that convey deportment or manner over the years that have governed my behavior.

- "A Horse, A Horse, My kingdom for a Horse!" (The first line of the Shakespeare play *Richard III*, Act 5).
- and ye shall know the truth and the truth shall make you free. John (8:32)
- "To thine own self be true" (*Hamlet*, Act 5)
- "Hindsight is knowing where you have been, foresight is knowing where you are going, and Insight is knowing when you've gone too far."
- In my days and before, we carried out bourbon on our hips; today they carry their guns on their hips.
- How to come out a winner while betting horse races? The answer: Bet heavy on the *winners* and light on the *losers*!

Writ by hand.

-No ghost writers-

I urge all of you who have read this to leave a written legacy for those that follow.

—John Sutton Jr.

America's Greatest Race

On the first Saturday in May, a major event takes place
where three-year-olds compete in a champion race.
Owners carry the hopes and colors of their honed thoroughbreds
with thoughts of winning the big one pulsing in their heads.

It began in Louisville, KY, in May of eighteen seventy-five
to match young champions with horses then alive.
It challenged all comers and grew huge through the years
and now stand unequaled and has hardly any peers.

To "Run for the Roses, you've got to be A-one, able and good
with preps all around and the "Bluegrass" or the "Wood."
They gather by the dozen to compete in this classic quest
to prove their stamina in this first-time mile-and-a-quarter test.

The greatest horses and jockeys all vie for the crown
as well as breeders who aspire to gain instant renown.
All of the owners and trainers set their sights on this race
and have conditioned their steeds to withstand the torrid pace.

It takes vets, walkers, grooms, and a whole lot of luck
and risks aplenty to get a big bang for your buck.
The bettor needs confidence, intuition, and logic for sure
to handicap their choice and for winning there is no cure.

If you haven't seen this spectacle yet, it's a <u>must</u> to be there
to feel the thrill of betting on your pick if you dare.
Select your choice and whether you wager a deuce or a fin,
if your fortunate enough to win, you'll be as happy as sin.

All the names above the portals, plus the dams and the sires,
gained fame and strode into history beneath the *"Twin Spires."*

It's all about going the distance and carrying the pounds
early in the season, devoid of injury, and at Churchill Downs.

As tens of thousands gather to see the horses of note
from the barn they're led to the paddock by the tote.
To be readied and saddled under the eye of the host
with jockeys up, the crowd awaits the call to the post.

To the strains of "My Old Kentucky
Home," they approach the gate
all the preparation and talent now is in the hands of fate.
The crowd is hushed before erupting in a thunderous roar,
"They're off and running, and it affects you down to the core.

Whether you choose the exotics or win, place, or show,
if you cash, I'll bet ya you'll want the world to know.
And when you're standing tall in that smiling line,
everyone about will know that you've done just fine.

This race has been summed up in many a famous quote,
but anyone present could voice something of note.
And you can bet your bottom dollar that I for one
will attend the next **Kentucky Derby** when it's all said and done!

John Sutton, 2000
Copyrighted

John S. Sutton Sr.
August 23, 1902 – July 23, 1980

During the heat of the summer, a boy arrived on the scene,
born to a woman of wisdom and a man named Gene.
Through faith and persistence, they honed a razor-sharp mind
and weren't satisfied till he was one-of-a-kind.

Nurtured by nature with more than one promising feature,
he expanded and grew on a prayer and a teacher.
Always one step ahead, there was nothing to be feared
for by darned and by granny was the way he was reared.

All through school at the head of his class,
he could wind up his motor and give it the gas.
During that day and time when two bits was a dollar,
he was accurate and fast with the mind of a scholar.

Ability and fate necessitated an apparent role to fulfill,
so he bade all farewell for a boarding house in Louisville.
With confidence, enthusiasm, and zeal that was undeniable,
he warmed to the task the beckoned at Old Reliable.

After a full head of steam and his feet hit the ground,
a family to support, he was duty-bound.
Through prohibition, depression, and wars that were risky
he matured with age like good bourbon whiskey.

A lifetime of entries revealed very few debits;
in the right-hand column, a whole lot of credits.
His prowess in his field was acknowledged hither and yon
as a special accountant known as personable John.

D & J
August 23, 1970

John Sutton Sr. (Age 63 – Father)

All About Mother
Ruth Roby Sutton
November 6, 1899 – May 13, 1992

The firstborn girl of Joseph Roby and Ann Bean,
a beautiful person and daughter they did wean.
He was a well-to-do farmer and was respected by all;
she was an aristocratic mother of five who stood tall.

Born on Nov. 6, '99, and the nineteenth century was winding down
in a small community in Nelson Country near Bardstown.
Her mother's kin were prominent citizens who were duty-bound
that contributed generously to their neighbors all around.

When she was nine years of age, her mother passed away,
and she assumed her adult duties in a responsible way.
Her father, he did promise to follow Annie's last requests
and to provide for the children in a way that was best.

It was then and there that her character was molded.
She carried on religiously when others may have folded.
Completed her schooling and to Nazareth she did go;
when her father passed on, she heard the cold wind blow.

Gathering her strengths, she entered St. Mary's Nursing School;
there was little time for dreaming and for trying to be <u>cool</u>.
She kept council with her siblings as she completed her term,
emerging young and vivacious with her convictions firm.

Now an RN, she wed John Sutton in '26 on Thanksgiving Day,
and it was evident right away she'd have something to say.
In the next ten years, they produced three children to rear,
and she tackled those multiple tasks with hardly any fear.

Most people want their accolades, but her horn she didn't toot,
and from her beliefs sprouted that <u>seed,</u> which has taken root.
Her zest for living was a product of tenacious will,
a trait, developed early on, that enabled her to climb any hill.

She persisted in doing the right thing, for goodness sake,
and it did her heart good to give rather than to take.
If your nose is in the air, you must keep your feet on the ground;
adopt her attitude, for its an idea you can get your arms around.

She insisted you break bread at her home and drink from her cup
and if you think of giving up, think of her and give it up.
In our mind, we thought Ruth Evelyn Roby would go on forever,
and it was out good fortune to have been tied to her tether.

Later, she enjoyed playing bridge and going to the race track;
somehow she came up a winner and for that she had a knack.
Her enthusiasm was such that even if you lost, you won;
just reshuffle the deck and deal, or bet and give it another run.

Let us reminisce, dream a little, and turn back the years,
to recall the songs she sang that now brings us to tears.
Looking back over the years, we know who held it all together
and who never took credit, but was a real life go-getter.

She was a social phenom who fancied what was brand-new,
which was a God-given gift that personified her point of view.
She had beauty, class, style, and a special way like no other,
a one-of-a-kind and not just because she's our mother.

John Sutton, 2000

Caption – Ruth Sutton (Circa 1970's – Mother)

*Caption – Ruth Sutton (Mother) – 1963 – with
grandchildren – Deborah, Eugene & Thomas*

John S. Sutton Jr. (the Poet's Bio)
July 12, 1931 –

Born in July '31, the firstborn son of Sutton and Ruth,
    he was unusually quiet to tell you the truth.
He went about his business in a matter-of-fact manner,
    little did anyone know he was a detailed planner.

He was wild as a deer and wasn't averse to having fun;
    to play hard was his work and his work was never done.
    He had not a clue what he wanted most to be,
    but he knew that to listen and to learn was the key.

An injury while young helped instill purpose and drive,
    and that was enough to make him glad to be alive.
On through St. X and U of L with a hop and a skip,
    he made it look easy and took very little lip.

That he didn't need much was as clear as a bell,
but before you can go to heaven, you have to go through hell.
    You gotta wanna sacrifice if you want to score, and
    he had plenty of determination and much, much more.

He's a bachelor of arts and master in math,
    and he couldn't be swayed from pursuing his path.
He was a leader, took chances, but stayed within the law,
    and was the first to defend, but would settle for a draw.

In the army during the Korean War he did serve,
    a new life and married simultaneously took some nerve.
With responsibilities galore, his feet hit the ground;
    a family to raise, there were solutions to be found.

Manager of quality control and purchasing VP,
    and he did it without catering to the powers that be.

His deductive reasoning made him a cool cat;
after thirty-five years, he retired and was glad of that.

With intuitive investments, he acquired funds and stocks
and now no longer frets about holes in his socks.
He'll allow nothing to count him out or down,
for his physical strength was the star in his crown.

To the KY Derby with his father he did go;
he begged and pleaded to attend the big show.
Starting in 1940, they beat the fave and was a big deal,
only one on earth to attend for eighty-two years, and that's unreal.

John S Sutton Jr

Jo-Ann (Sutton) Gosnell
October 29, 1927 – November 25, 2004

She was the firstborn child of Sutton and Ruth,
a girl that was gifted and that's the truth!
Fast off the mark, a very quick study,
you better believe she was no fuddy-duddy.

A child of God, she was destined to be keen.
She made it her business to be part of the scene.
She took her chances and made it all fit
and put it together with beauty and wit.

Through schools early on then Presentation,
she forged right though with no hesitation.
Popular and attractive with lots of pride,
it was a snap for her, and she took it in stride.

By now she was stunning with a great personality
with charm and class and a dose of joviality.
No obstacle too great, she had plenty to sell,
with thoughts of a family she married Gosnell.

Now two children named Linda and Jeff,
the course was set with no turning left.
The daughter a barrister, the son a banker,
needless to say, both of them thank her.

And now it seems she's just getting started;
with senses honed sharp, she can't be thwarted.
Most all of us are searching for a good time;
she's a must for a party that no one can mime.

Of laughter and words, she had no equal;
she keeps us waiting for the next sequel.

Let it be known throughout this here land
that neither money nor power can match JoAnn.

John Sutton
1997

Jo-Ann Sutton Gosnell

Doris Jean (Hornung) Sutton
June 24, 1932 –

On the 24th of June, a new day was dawning
A baby girl was born to Magdalen and Hornung.
You could tell early on she had lots to say
and was a bright little kid with a very special way.

Mind like a sponge, she was a very quick learner
It was easy for her to turn up the burner.
She applied herself; yes, you could say she was heady
and approached every task in a way that was steady.

At the top of her class she had a hefty IQ
and proved that fact with the highest average too.
Completed business school regimen in half the time
and continued that scenario on down the line.

Mild mannered and pleasant, she was coming on strong
and persisted in her view to do very little wrong.
She was attractive and fine, and oh! What a catch!
I knew at once that I had met my match.

Married now, she went with John to Fort Sill
and impressed the brass with her ability and skill.
With thoughts of a family and becoming a mom,
she bore three children Deborah, Francis, and Tom.

Now she opted to test her will and her mettle
and, of course, for second, she would not settle.
She used her logic to tame a megabyte blizzard
and became a systems analyst and a computer wizard.

One for the ages, she's as great as they come.
For heaven's sake! God only knows where she came from.

And yes, my friends, it's a matter of fact
that all through the years, she's been a class act.

With that behind her, she'd rather give than to take
and help others in need and reside down by the lake.
Never before has the planet earth ever seen
a woman as nice and neat as sweet Doris Jean.

John Sutton

Doris Jean Sutton

Deborah Ann (Sutton) Sims
September 5, 1956 –

Arrived on September 5, '56, to Doris and John,
and yes! The mega-jackpot we had won.
A 7.5 lb. bright-eyed girl with auburn hair,
we knew at once this bird was rare.

A beautiful person both inside and out,
she had a special way, there was no doubt.
She loved to work jigsaw puzzles at three,
and her skill was a sight to see.

Grew up fast with two brothers to fight,
she was of a mind to do what was right.
Like her mom, she attended Presentation school
and practiced the age-old golden rule.

She knew early on her destiny to fulfill
and got married to Sims and said, "I will."
Amber D. and Brandon M. were soon to be,
and they were a duo that suited her to a T.

We all must live with the cards we are dealt,
but she solved <u>whatever</u> by tightening her belt.
Don't while away your time, so say she,
but make the best of it or just let it be.

Her endeavors were too many to mention;
her modest style is not to seek attention.
A take-charge person became her special trait
and treated all the same regardless of their fate.

Now she tends to her flock and her siblings too
and keeps them on track regardless of what they do.

She's mastered a lost art—and wow! Can she cook,
and it is all <u>well done</u> without even reading the book.

An outstanding daughter and a mother, you bet,
and the twinkle in her eye says she's not done yet.
With charm, grace, and beauty, she can't be measured,
and she's our gal that will be forever treasured.

She accomplished her mission of genuine love
by using the characteristics listed above.
She can take it or leave it, and to hell with the latest
all of us know who is really the greatest.

Mom and Dad
September 5, 2011

Deborah (Circa – 1974 – Senior Year – Daughter)

Francis Eugene Sutton
April 24, 1958 –

Born April 24th, his grandfather being his namesake,
to Doris and John, in the Ville who baked that cake.
The middle child of a diverse brood all close in age,
to know he was different didn't require a sage.

As a young boy, he was always ahead of the rest;
he had the whole package, and yes! He was the best.
All through school his sights were set and was on the right track,
he seemed to have a work ethic with no turning back.

Whether to the crack of the bat or the sound of the swish,
he easily did what most others could only wish.
That he took them to task, there was no doubt,
when a bombed from all over it was light's out.

He showed his moxie as an expert barrel kicker,
and that's loads better than being a cotton picker.
He punched his card daily through thick and thin
and showed what he had done and where he had been.

He had done with and he had done without
and lived through both with ease, there was no doubt.
He had his ups and downs but came out on top;
he studied the zodiac and gave it some pop.

We know perseverance is a big key to good luck
and make sure you obtain the most bang for your buck.
He works, thinks, and plays by the numbers, thus far
and it's not if, but when he catches that shooting star.

He is a pro at winning the lottery and the races,
which is determined by putting his brain through the paces.

This knowledge of dates and number is beyond the pale
and this rare kind of acumen is not up for sale.

It's the measure of a man to withstand a trial.
He survived adversity and won by a mile.
He is strong and tall, and his sense are keen.
Yes! We're talking about our son named *Gene*.

Francis Eugene Sutton

Thomas Gerard Sutton
August 12, 1959 – February 16, 2021

Born on August 12th in the heat of the summer,
he was in like a lion and was an up-and-comer.
The youngest of three, named the same as the apostle Thomas,
and you could see in his eyes that he had lots of promise

He was blessed with good health and an intuitive bean,
and he had a good ear and his senses were keen.
He made us laugh with his talent as a mimic,
and he did it with ease and was never a cynic.

He was a good listener and indeed a quick study,
and you can be sure he was no fuddy-duddy.
He had a knack for phrasing and poetry skills
and could connect things together without any frills.

He used the Weider program to sculpt his frame
and squats and curls here part of his game.
We recall the one-arm-chin-up and crack of the bat!
And if that didn't impress, he could take you to the mat.

He grew strong, like an oak, and was standing tall;
and then, like Humpty Dumpty, he had a great fall.
Just to have survived was a miraculous feat;
to overcome this, it took courage to withstand the heat.

The rehabilitation venue took determination and grit,
but he didn't hesitate even for one little bit.
He awoke from a coma and could barely talk;
like the phoenix, he rose up and embraced the walk.

Thinking of the future, he had to get up and go,
so he got up and went by never saying *no*.

Perseverance and moderation are life's big keys,
and a setback or two couldn't bring him to his knees.

His legacy will be turning negatives into positives,
rather than giving into many asinine alternatives.
He took steps to go forward in lieu of asking why,
and his family knows he's one <u>helluva</u> guy.

Mom and Dad
August 12, 2015

Thomas Gerard Sutton

Amber Dawn (Sutton) Sims
August 16, 1980 –

Born to James F. Sims and Deborah A. Sutton
on August 16, 1980, healthy and cute as a button.
If you've ever seen the sunrise on a clear spring day,
that's how she acquired her name, by the way.

A combination of brains and beauty was she,
which seems to describe her attributes to a tee.
Early on she displayed ways that were upbeat
that could face tribulations and take the heat.

Under any condition, she can and will hold her own,
pleasant and nice or, if need be, bad to the bone.
If you are choosing sides, you got to be on her team,
then you'll be glad to know that you're on the beam.

She grew like a sunflower and went on to school
and made high marks, and OMG! Was she cool.
Her mind was made up and was determined to excel,
and it all ended up with a degree from U of L.

Meanwhile, she used her time to work for the money
to support herself, and Oh! Was she a honey.
If it comes to pass that you would be friend or foe,
you better be ready to contend with her mojo!

It's what you know, and not where you've been.
Who cares! As long as you have a valid sheepskin.
She honed her skills on the computer for sure
and took a tech job with UPS due to the lure.

She was promoted to super after a very short time
and toiled night and day and was one of a kind.

She purchased a nearby condo in which to reside
while seeking the next tidal wave on which to ride.

You can look around the bend or maybe too far,
but right under our nose was our shining star.
When the show concludes and the curtains are drawn,
there in the limelight is our Amber Dawn.

Grandma and Grandpa
August 16, 2018

Amber (Grand daughter - circa 2012)

Brandon Michael (Sutton) Sims
January 6, 1986 –

He was born on January 6th during midwinter;
you could see in his eyes that he was a winner.
Deborah Sutton on the distaff; James Sims the sire,
and the result was a son who would win at the wire.

After toiling at the movies, he went to work for Best Buy,
and it was evident to them that he was their guy.
He wed beautiful Ashlee Davis, and the beat goes on;
now a husband and father, which pleased him a ton.

He was never one for idle frivolous chatter,
which is usually the sign of lots of gray matter.
Scientist have long looked for the missing link,
but his is the chain that <u>binds</u> that's written in ink.

There's no doubt about it that he's a Cardinals fan,
and he can recite the stats down to the last man.
He can fly by the seat of his pants or go by the book,
somehow or another, he always knew what it took.

He's heady, ready, steady, willing, and able
to tackle whatever and can even fix your cable.
You can't underestimate the size of his heart,
it's a matter of fact, and that's what sets him apart.

The good book says "As ye sow, so shall ye reap,"
it's his modus operandi, and it's his to keep.
We know that perseverance is the key to success,
and it's this characteristic that he doth possess.

Along came baby Alyvia that changed the ball game;
she was a first stringer and life would never be the same.

There's no doubt his parents and grandparents are proud
due to his special mojo that stands out from the crowd.

As we travel through the trials of modern-day life,
so did our ancestors, who were fraught with rife.
He is aware of those ordeals, and that's a fact,
which is rare these days, and that's why he a class act.

Who you gonna call on when the going gets tough?
Certainly <u>not</u> the pretenders or some powder puff.
To hell with the celebs, wannabes, and self-serving hacks,
we'll <u>take</u> Brandon Michael over all the Jills and Jacks.

Grandma and Grandpa
January 6, 2020

Brandon (Circa 2018 – Grandson)

John & Doris – Circa – 2006 – 60ᵗʰ Wedding Anniversary

Whiskey Barrel Head – Retirement Gift

*100 year old Churchill Downs - Willow Wood Chair –
Used at Churchill Downs in the Clubhouse – Outside.*

Collection of Kentucky Derby glasses – 1940 – 2021

*Large Mouth Bass Trophy from Fishing Trip on
Lake Hatchineha – 8 LBS 8 OZ*

Printed in the United States
by Baker & Taylor Publisher Services